HATCHED AND PATCHED'S

Some Kind
* O F *
Wonderful

Anni Downs

KANSAS CITY STAR
QUILTS
Continuing the Tradition

Hatched and Patched's
Some Kind of Wonderful

By Anni Downs
Editor: Kimber Mitchell
Design: Amy Robertson
Photography: Aaron T. Leimkuehler
Illustration: Eric Sears
Technical Editor: Christina DeArmond
Production assistance: Jo Ann Groves

Published by:
Kansas City Star Books
1729 Grand Blvd.
Kansas City, Missouri, USA 64108

First edition, first printing
ISBN: 978-1-935362-83-8

Library of Congress Control Number:
2011924702

Printed in the United States of America
By Walsworth Publishing Co.,
Marceline, MO

The Quilter's Home Page

About the Author

Anni Downs has loved to sew for as long as she can remember. She realized her dream of working with fabric when she left a computer graphics career in Brisbane, Australia, to live in Coonamble, 17 years ago. There, she found herself surrounded by an inspiring community of sewers and began designing quilt patterns for a local mail-order patchwork company. In 1996, Anni formed her own patchwork design business, Hatched and Patched. Since then, she has designed more than 100 patterns and self-published eight books. Handwork is Anni's greatest passion, and when she travels, she always has a stitching project in hand. She enjoys spending most of her time exploring the many possibilities of fabric and other mediums.

Anni lives in Bathurst, Australia, with her husband Pete, daughter Samantha, son Tim, and a crazy cat (Munch) and dog (Tilly). She owns a quilt shop, The Home Patch, located in an historical inn. *Some Kind of Wonderful* is her first book with Kansas City Star Quilts.

Acknowledgments

Writing a book is a collaborative process and I have many people to thank for helping to make it possible.

Thanks so much to my husband Pete for taking over the cooking duties when I'm under deadline as well as the constant care you show when I'm at a crisis point. You are definitely my rock!

Thanks to my two children Samantha and Tim, who have to put up with a constantly messy dining room table, which often serves as my substitute studio.

Thanks to Margaret and Michelle, who work in my shop and often serve as springboards for my design ideas. You are forever patient and ask for so little despite having to fend for yourselves when I'm busy working on designs.

Thanks to Helen Vanderhel for sewing the Snuggle quilt and to Belinda Betts who drops everything to quilt my projects when my deadlines are tight. You always go out of your way to create something spectacular.

Thanks also to the talented Kansas City Star Quilts team:

Doug Weaver and Diane McLendon for giving me the opportunity to write this book.

The wonderful Kimber Mitchell, my diligent editor who has held my hand from the beginning of this process.

Thanks also to Amy, my designer; Aaron, my photographer; Eric, my illustrator; and Christina, my technical editor. It was a treat to work with such a gifted team of professionals.

Contents

Introduction

When designing the projects for this book, I wanted to capture everything that I love about my life. My greatest love is purely being at home with my husband and children. I also enjoy spending time with my friends and extended family, gardening, cooking, reading, and, of course, sewing. The projects in this book reflect those many passions and use my favorite sewing techniques and materials. I love the simple pleasures of hand stitching, and I'm drawn to all things natural—wools, linens, and hand-dyed threads.

I have sewn for as long as I can remember, but it wasn't until my children were born that I delved whole-heartedly into hand stitching. As a busy mom, I didn't have much free time, so I found the best way to carve out stitching time was to have portable projects that I could carry with me wherever I went. To help keep your stitching supplies organized while on the go, I have included a whimsical sewing case, pincushion, and needle book in this book.

As much as I love being at home, I do enjoy exploring the countryside both near and far. Whenever we have an opportunity, my family and I escape to the beach or the mountains. We love to visit friends and explore new and interesting places. For those of you who share my fondness for traveling, I've included a host of travel companions to make your adventures more enjoyable.

Nothing compares to the joy of searching flea markets and secondhand stores for something unique. I remember for my 21st birthday, my grandmother gave me money to buy something special like a handbag or piece of jewelry. Instead, I went to a junk shop and bought an old desk, a bed, and a chair. I still have that old chair and every time I use it I am reminded of my gorgeous grandmother. Because I love to explore interesting shops, I just had to include a handy bag and coin purse, perfect for taking along on your shopping trips.

I am one of those lucky people who can honestly say I don't want for anything. The idea for this book originated with that sense of happiness in mind. It is a celebration of all things wonderful. I know many of you share my passions—relaxing at home, exploring familiar and new places, shopping with friends, and, of course, stitching a quilt or other fun project. I hope these whimsical projects will bring you as much joy as they have me. Before you get started, please refer to pages 8-9 for some general sewing guidelines for all the projects as well as basic pointers on appliqué and hand stitching.

Anni

Stitching Primer

GENERAL INSTRUCTIONS

❋ Read all instructions carefully before starting the projects.
❋ Fabric quantities are for 42"-wide, 100% cotton fabrics.
❋ Use a ¼" seam allowance unless otherwise noted.
❋ Sew fabrics with right sides together unless otherwise noted.
❋ Press seams toward darker fabric and/or in the direction that creates the least bulk.

APPLIQUÉ INSTRUCTIONS

Preparing Your Appliqué

1. I recommend adding an extra inch to the background fabric cutting dimensions listed in this book to allow for distortion while appliquéing. You can then trim the block to its exact size after it has been appliquéd.
2. Using a light box or window, place the appliqué background fabric over the appliqué/stitchery template.
3. For ease of appliqué placement, use a soft pencil or wash-out pen to lightly trace some key elements of the appliqué design on the appliqué background fabric.
4. Using a Pigma pen or pencil, trace any stitchery components, including any stems or words, on the appliqué background fabric.
5. To create your appliqué templates, you can either trace each appliqué design on freezer paper before cutting them out (do not add a seam allowance to these shapes) or you can trace the images directly on your chosen appliqué fabric, using a light box or window and a wash-out marker or pencil. If using freezer-paper templates, iron them to the right side of your fabric, then trace around each template with a water-soluble pen or pencil. Add a scant ¼" seam allowance before cutting out each template.
6. To help the appliqué lay flat, clip any concave seams to the drawn line.

Appliquéing the Blocks

1. For a more traditional look, I used needleturn appliqué for most of the projects in this book, but feel free to use the appliqué method you like best. If you opt for raw-edge appliqué, please note that all appliqué images must be reversed.
2. Pin and stitch the appliqué pieces to the appliqué background fabric.
3. When stitching, use a thread that blends with each appliqué piece.
4. Using the point of your needle or pressing with your finger, turn the seam allowance under at the drawn line as you go.
5. Slipstitch the appliqué pieces into place.

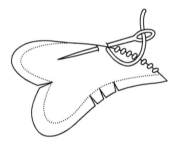

WOOL APPLIQUÉ

For small appliqué pieces, I prefer to use a double-sided fusible web to stabilize the wool.

1. Trace the reverse image on the fusible web, leaving about an ⅛" seam allowance around each piece.
2. Cut out all the pieces just outside the pencil line.
3. Iron the fusible web paper to the wrong side of the wool and cut directly on the pencil line.
4. Peel the paper from the other side of the fusible web and position all parts of the appliqué design on the background fabric, overlapping where necessary. Pin in place.
5. Using one strand of embroidery floss and a whipstitch or blanket stitch, appliqué pieces to the background fabric.

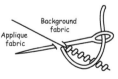

Whipstitch (ws)

TRANSFERRING STITCHERY DESIGNS TO FABRIC

1. With a wash-out pencil, draw the cutting line on the background fabric. Do not cut out the drawn cutting line until the stitching is complete as the stitching can distort the fabric.
2. Using a Pigma pen and a light source, trace the image on the background fabric.
3. Referring to the stitch key below, stitch the design. The codes in parentheses refer to the type of stitches used (i.e. bs=backstitch).

STITCH KEY

The projects in this book use several hand stitches. To create them, see the diagrams below.

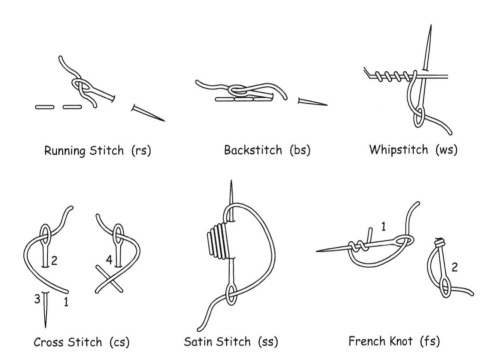

Running Stitch (rs)   Backstitch (bs)   Whipstitch (ws)

Cross Stitch (cs)   Satin Stitch (ss)   French Knot (fs)

My Favorite Things Quilt

Finished size: 61½" x 69" • Designed and made by Anni Downs • Quilted by Belinda Betts

I adore many of life's simple pleasures—being in the garden, watching the birds and butterflies, and just taking in the sunshine. I also love sharing a story or two with friends over some delicious food and a hot chocolate. One of my other favorite things to do is spending a day at the beach while indulging in an ice cream cone to cool down. And of course, I adore being at home where I can sit around in my old jeans and stitch, read, or play a game with my children. To me, these simple joys represent life at its best. You'll find these whimsical themes and more in this lighthearted quilt filled with all the things I love.

FABRIC REQUIREMENTS
Appliqué backgrounds, border strips, and patchwork sections:
- 6 yards total of 8 assorted cream/beige prints

Appliqué blocks and patchwork sections:
- 16 fat eighths of assorted colored prints (I used a brown solid, brown star, brown/beige geometric, yellow print, cream solid, raspberry with cream berry, lighter raspberry with beige leaf, pink spot, pink stripe, light green spot, green stripe, dark green spot, light blue floral, blue stripe, blue with brown leaf and teal floral)

Binding:
- ¾ yard brown print

DMC embroidery floss:
- Light brown (167), Brown (869), Blue (926), Green (3012), Dark gray/brown (3021), and Raspberry (3721)

CUTTING INSTRUCTIONS
Remember to add an extra inch to the background block cutting dimensions below to allow for distortion while appliquéing. Then trim them to size once the appliqué and stitchery is complete. I cut three appliqué background blocks from each of the eight cream/beige print squares listed in the fabric requirements.

From cream/beige prints, cut:
- 4 or 5 – 2" strips the width of fabric from each print for a total of 35 strips for the borders and columns (Cut these **before** the appliqué background blocks)
- 1 – 7½" x 8½" rectangle for the Patty Cakes background block
- 1 – 7½" x 9½" rectangle for the Umbrella background block
- 2 – 7½" squares for the Tea Cup and Suitcase background blocks
- 1 – 7½" x 12½" rectangle for the Old Blue Jeans background block
- 1 – 5½" square for the Chocolates background block
- 1 – 5½" x 18½" rectangle for the Daisy background block
- 1 – 5½" x 10½" rectangle for the Ice Cream background block
- 1 – 5½" x 7½" rectangle for the Hot Chocolate background block
- 1 – 5½" x 8½" rectangle for the Book background block

❋ 3 – 8½" x 14½" rectangles for the House, Tree, and Best Friends background blocks

❋ 2 – 7½" x 8½" rectangles for the Flowers and Cat background blocks

❋ 2 – 8½" squares for the Rainbow and Shoes background blocks

❋ 1 – 8½" x 12½" rectangle for the Sewing background block

❋ 3 – 6½" squares for the Butterfly, Bird, and Present background blocks

❋ 1 – 6½" x 7½" rectangle for the Heart background block

❋ 1 – 6½" x 8½" rectangle for the Sun background block

❋ 1 – 6½" x 12½" rectangle for the Chair background block

❋ 82 – 2½" squares for the patchwork sections and columns

❋ 130 – 1½" squares for the patchwork sections and columns

From assorted colored prints, cut:

❋ 133 – 1½" squares for the patchwork sections and columns

❋ 29 – 2" squares for the patchwork sections and columns

❋ 2 – 1½" x 1¾" rectangles for the Sewing block's two-patch unit

❋ 2 – 1" squares for the Sewing block's Log Cabin unit

❋ 2 – 1" x 1½" rectangles for the Sewing block's Log Cabin unit

❋ 2 – 1" x 2" rectangles for the Sewing block's Log Cabin unit

❋ 2 – 1" x 2½" rectangles for the Sewing block's Log Cabin unit

❋ 1 – 1" x 3" rectangle for the Sewing block's Log Cabin unit

❋ 2 – 2⅛" brown print squares for the Sewing block's Broken Dishes unit

❋ 2 – 2⅛" blue print squares for the Sewing block's Broken Dishes unit

❋ Appliqué templates on pages 78-103. For color cues, refer to page 15.

From brown print, cut:

❋ 7 – 2½" strips the width of fabric for binding

SEWING INSTRUCTIONS

Appliqué blocks

1. Referring to the appliqué placement guides on pages 78-103, appliqué pieces to the background fabrics. You will make a total of 24 blocks. **Please note the black lines are the appliqué and the gray lines are the stitchery.**

2. Referring to the stitch guide on page 13 and the gray lines on the templates on pages 78-103, stitch the designs for each block. Anni personalized her Suitcase block with her name but you can leave it blank or stitch your own name.

"SEWING" APPLIQUÉ BLOCK

To complete the Sewing appliqué block, you will need to sew a Log Cabin block, a Broken Dishes block, and a two-patch unit.

Log Cabin block:

1. Sew a 1" dark beige print square to a 1" raspberry print square.

2. Referring to the first diagram below, sew a 1" x 1½" dark beige print rectangle to the unit from Step 1.

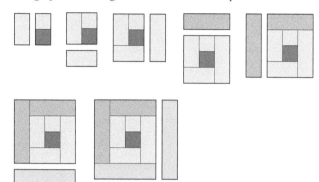

3. Referring to the second diagram above, sew a 1" x 1½" light green print rectangle to the unit from Step 2.

4. Referring to the third diagram above, sew a 1" x 2" light green print rectangle to the unit from Step 3.

5. Referring to the fourth diagram above, sew a 1" x 2" pink print rectangle to the unit from Step 4.

6. Referring to the fifth diagram above, sew a 1" x 2½" pink print rectangle to the unit from Step 5.

7. Referring to the sixth diagram above, sew a 1" x 2½" teal print rectangle to the unit from Step 6.

8. Referring to the seventh diagram above, sew a 1" x 3" teal print rectangle to the unit from Step 7. The resulting unit should measure 3" square.

Broken Dishes block

1. Referring to the first diagram below, use a permanent pen, pencil or chalk marker to draw a diagonal line once from corner to corner on the wrong side of the 2 – 2⅛" brown print squares.

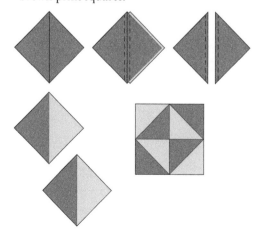

STITCH GUIDE

Use two strands for all the flosses listed here. See the stitch key on page 9 for the types of stitches referenced in parentheses.

Patty Cakes block:
- Words – DMC 869 (bs)

Umbrella block:
- Pole and spikes – DMC 3021 (bs)
- Words – DMC 869 (bs)

Tea Cup block:
- Steam lines – DMC 167 (bs)
- Words – DMC 869 (bs)

Old Blue Jeans block:
- Pockets, zipper, and belt loops – DMC 926 (bs)
- Crosses on legs – DMC 926 (cs)
- Peace sign – DMC 3021 (bs)
- Words – DMC 869 (bs)

Suitcase block:
- Tag string – DMC 169 (bs)
- Words – DMC 869 (bs)

Chocolates block:
- Cherry on top right chocolate – DMC 3721 (ss)
- All other chocolates – DMC 3021 (bs & rs)
- Words – DMC 869 (bs)

Daisy block:
- Stem – DMC 3012 (bs)
- Word – DMC 869 (bs)

Ice Cream block:
- Words – DMC 869 (bs)

Hot Chocolate block:
- Steam lines – DMC 167 (rs)
- Words – DMC 869 (bs)

Book block:
- Words on book – DMC 3021 (bs)
- Crosses on spine – DMC 3021 (cs)
- Spine line and other words – DMC 869 (bs)
- Paper line – DMC 167 (bs)

House block:
- Tree trunks and words – DMC 869 (bs)

Flowers block:
- Words – DMC 869 (bs)
- Flower stems – DMC 3012 (bs)

Tree block:
- Bird leg – DMC 167 (bs)
- Bird beak – DMC 167 (ss)
- Words, cat tail, cat whiskers, and cat legs – DMC 869 (bs)
- Cat nose – DMC 3021 (ss)
- Cat mouth – DMC 3021 (bs)
- Cat and bird eyes – DMC 3021 (fk)

Rainbow block:
- Words – DMC 869 (bs)
- Flower stem – DMC 3012 (bs)

Sewing block:
- Scissor detail and pin shafts – DMC 646 (bs)
- Words, circle, and cross on 4th button – DMC 869 (bs)
- Spots on 4th button – DMC 869 (fk)
- 3rd and 8th pin head – DMC 926 (ss)
- 2nd, 5th, and 6th pin head – DMC 3012 (ss)
- 3rd button circle and line – DMC 3012 (bs)
- Spots on 3rd button – DMC 3012 (fk)
- "PINS" wording, ruler measurements and numbers, and lines on 2nd and 5th buttons – DMC 3021 (bs)
- Spots on 2nd and 5th buttons – 3021 (fk)
- Crosses on pincushion, lines and crosses left of scissors, and line on first button – DMC 3721 (bs)
- Spots on 1st button – DMC 3721 (fk)
- 1st, 4th and 7th pin heads – DMC 3721 (ss)

Shoes block:
- Words – DMC 869 (bs)

Butterfly block:
- Antennae – DMC 167 (bs)
- Words – DMC 869 (bs)
- Eyes – DMC 3021 (fk)

Cat block:
- "Pet cat" words and whiskers – DMC 869 (bs)
- Cat mouth and "Meow" and "Munch" words – DMC 3021 (bs)
- Eyes – DMC 3021 (fk)

Best Friends block:
- Hair and legs on left girl, legs on right girl – DMC 167 (bs)
- Words and shoe heels – DMC 869 (bs)
- Eyes – DMC 869 (fk)
- Shoelaces on left shoe – DMC 926 (cs)
- Hair on right girl – DMC 3021 (bs)
- Lips and shoe laces on right shoes – DMC 3721 (bs)

Bird block:
- Words – DMC 869 (bs)
- Eye – DMC 3021 (fk)
- Legs – DMC 3721 (bs)

Sun block:
- Ray lines – DMC 167 (bs)
- Scroll on sun appliqué – DMC 167 (rs)
- Words – DMC 869 (bs)

Chair block:
- Words – DMC 869 (bs)

Heart block:
- Words – DMC 869 (bs)

Present block:
- Words – DMC 869 (bs)
- Ribbon – DMC 3721 (bs)

2. Referring to the second diagram on page 12 under Broken Dishes block, layer one 2⅛" brown print square on top of one 2⅛" blue print square with right sides together. Sew a scant ¼" seam on both sides of the drawn line. Repeat this step for the other pair of squares.

3. Referring to the third diagram on page 12 under Broken Dishes block, cut on the drawn line.

4. Each pair of squares will make 2 – 1¾" unfinished half-square triangles, as shown in the fourth diagram on page 12 under Broken Dishes block, for a total of 4. Trim the excess fabric on the corners.

5. Referring to the fifth diagram on page 12 under Broken Dishes block, sew the four half-square triangles together. The resulting unit should measure 3" square.

Two-patch unit

1. Sew a 1½" x 1¾" teal print rectangle to a 1½" x 1¾" brown print rectangle on the 1½" sides. The finished unit should measure 1½" x 3".

Finishing the Sewing appliqué block

1. Turn the raw edges of the Log Cabin block, Broken Dishes block, and two-patch unit under a ¼" and press.

2. Referring to the appliqué placement guide for the Sewing block on page 94, slipstitch the Log Cabin block, Broken Dishes block, and two-patch unit to the appliqué background fabric.

PATCHWORK SECTIONS

This quilt contains 27 different patchwork sections between the appliqué blocks.

1. Sew 129 – 1½" cream/beige print squares to 129 – 1½" assorted colored squares to create 129 two-patch units.

2. Sew together 54 of the two-patch units to create 27 four-patch units. You should now have a total of 75 two-patch units, 27 four-patch units, 1 – 1½" cream/beige print square, and 4 – 1½" assorted colored squares.

3. Sew a 2½" cream square to each side of a four-patch unit. Then sew a two-patch unit to the left of that unit. The resulting unit should measure 2½" x 7½". Sew this section to the top of the Patty Cakes block.

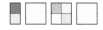

4. Sew a two-patch unit to a 2½" cream print square. Repeat twice. Then sew a 1½" colored square to the light print square of a two-patch unit. Join these four units. The resulting unit should measure 3½" x 7½". Sew this section to the bottom of the Patty Cakes block and the top of the Umbrella block.

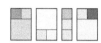

5. Sew a four-patch unit to the base of a 2½" cream print square; a two-patch unit to the top and bottom of a 2½" cream print square; 2 – 2½" cream print squares together; and 2 two-patch units together end to end. Join these four units. The resulting unit should measure 4½" x 7½". Sew this section to the base of the Umbrella block and the top of the Tea Cup block.

6. Sew a 2½" cream print square to each side of a two-patch unit. Then sew a four-patch unit to the right of that unit. The resulting unit should measure 2½" x 7½" inches. Sew this section to the base of the Tea Cup block and the top of the Old Blue Jeans block.

7. Sew a four-patch unit to the top of a 2½" cream print square; a two-patch unit to each side of a 2½" cream-print square; 2 – 2½" cream print squares together; and 2 two-patch units together end to end. Join these four units. The resulting unit should measure 4½" x 7½". Sew this section to the base of the Old Blue Jeans block and the top of the Suitcase block.

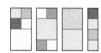

8. Sew a two-patch unit to a 2½" cream print square. Repeat twice. Sew a 1½" colored square to the light print square of a two-patch unit. Join these four units. The resulting unit should measure 3½" x 7½". Sew this section to the base of the Suitcase block. This completes the first column of the quilt. The column should measure 7½" x 61½".

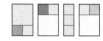

Patty Cakes

Chocolates

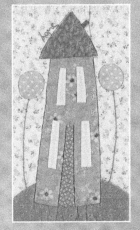

House

Sewing

Butterfly

Bird

Sun

Umbrella

Daisy

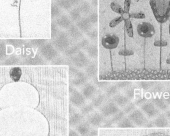

Flowers

Best Friends

Chair

Tea Cup

Ice Cream

Tree

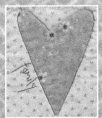

Shoes

Old Blue Jeans

Hot Chocolate

Heart

Suitcase

Book

Rainbow

Cat

Present

9. Sew 2 – 2½" cream print squares together. Then sew a two-patch unit to the right of that unit. The resulting unit should measure 2½" x 5½". Sew this section to the base of the Chocolates block and the top of the Daisy block.

10. Sew a four-patch unit to the base of a 2½" cream print square. Sew a two-patch unit to a 2½" cream print square and repeat once. Join these three units. The resulting unit should measure 4½" x 5½". Sew this section to the base of the Daisy block and the top of the Ice Cream block.

11. Sew a two-patch unit to a 2½" cream print square and repeat once. Sew a 1½" colored square to the cream end of a two-patch unit. Join these three units. The resulting unit should measure 3½" x 5½". Sew this section to the base of the Ice Cream block and the top of the Hot Chocolate block.

12. Sew 2 – 2½" cream print squares together. Then sew a two-patch unit to the left of that unit. The resulting unit should measure 2½" x 5½". Sew this section to the base of the Hot Chocolate block and the top of the Book block.

13. Sew a four-patch unit to the left of a 2½" cream print square. Then sew a two-patch unit to the right of the 2½" cream print square. The resulting unit should measure 2½" x 5½". Sew this section to the base of the Book block. This completes the second column of the quilt. The column should measure 5½" x 61½".

14. Sew a 2½" cream print square to each side of a two-patch unit. Then sew a two-patch unit to the left of that unit and a four-patch unit to its right. The resulting unit should measure 2½" x 8½". Sew this section to the top of the House block.

15. Sew a four-patch unit to the base of a 2½" cream print square, then sew a two-patch unit to the four-patch unit you just attached. Sew 2 – 2½" cream print squares together, then sew a two-patch unit to the top of that unit. Sew a four-patch unit to the top of a 2½" cream print square and a two-patch unit to the bottom. Sew a 2½" cream print square to each side of a two-patch unit. Join these four units. The resulting unit should measure 5½" x 8½". Sew this section to the base of the House block and top of the Flower block.

16. Sew a 2½" cream print square to each side of a two-patch unit. Then sew a 2½" cream print square to the left of that unit and a two-patch unit to its right. The resulting unit should measure 2½" x 8½". Sew this section to the base of the Flower block and the top of the Tree block.

17. Sew a two-patch unit to each side of a 2½" cream print square. Repeat once. Sew a four-patch unit to a 2½" cream print square. Repeat once. Join these four units. The resulting unit should measure 4½" x 8½". Sew this section to the base of the Tree block and the top of the Rainbow block.

18. Sew a 2½" cream print square to each side of a two-patch unit. Repeat once. Sew a four-patch unit to the top of a 2½" cream print square and a two-patch unit to its base. Repeat once. Join these four units. The resulting unit should measure 5½" x 8½". Sew this section to the base of the Rainbow block. This completes the third column of the quilt. The column should measure 8½" x 61½".

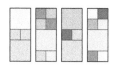

19. Sew a two-patch unit to a 2½" cream print square. Repeat twice. Sew a two-patch unit to a four-patch unit. Join these four units. The resulting unit should measure 3½" x 8½". Sew this section to the top of the Sewing block.

20. Sew a two-patch unit to each side of a 2½" cream print square. Repeat once. Sew a 2½" cream print square to a four-patch unit. Sew 2 – 2½" cream print squares together. Join these four units. The resulting unit should measure 4½" x 8½". Sew this section to the base of the Sewing block and the top of the Best Friends block.

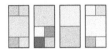

21. Sew a two-patch unit to a 2½" cream print square. Repeat five times, then sew these units together in pairs as shown below. Sew a 2½" cream print square to the top and bottom of a four-patch unit. Join these four units. The resulting unit should measure 6½" x 8½". Sew this section to the base of the Best Friends block and the top of the Shoe Block.

22. Sew a four-patch unit to a 2½" cream print square. Repeat twice. Sew a two-patch unit to each side of a 2½" cream print square. Join these four units. The resulting unit should measure 4½" x 8½". Sew this section to the base of the Shoe block and the top of the Cat block.

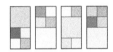

23. Sew a two-patch unit to a 2½" cream print square and repeat once; a two-patch unit to a four-patch unit; a 1½" light print square to a two-patch unit; and a 1½" dark print square to a two-patch unit. Join these five units. The resulting unit should measure 3½" x 8½". Sew this section to the base of the Cat block. This completes the fourth column of the quilt. The column should measure 8½" x 61½".

24. Sew a two-patch unit to a 2½" cream print square and repeat once. Sew a two-patch unit to a four-patch unit. Join these three units. The resulting unit should measure 3½" x 6½". Sew this section to base of the Butterfly block and the top of the Bird block.

25. Sew a two-patch unit to a four-patch unit. Then sew a two-patch unit to a 2½" cream print square and repeat once. Join these three units. The resulting unit should measure 3½" x 6½". Sew this section to the base of the Bird block and the top of the Sun block.

26. Sew a two-patch unit to each side of a 2½" cream print square. Sew a four-patch unit to a 2½" cream print square and repeat once. Join these three units. The resulting unit should measure 4½" x 6½". Sew this section to the base of the Sun block and the top of the Chair block.

27. Sew a two-patch unit to each side of a 2½" cream print square. Then sew a four-patch unit to the right of that unit. The resulting unit should measure 2½" x 6½". Sew this section to the base of the Chair block and the top of the Heart block.

28. Sew a 2½" cream print square to both sides of a two-patch unit. Then sew a two-patch unit to the right of that unit. The resulting unit should measure 2½" x 6½". Sew this section to the base of the Heart block and the top of the Present block.

29. Sew a four-patch unit to each side of a 2½" cream print square. The resulting unit should measure 2½" x 6½". Sew this section to the base of the Present block. This completes the fifth column. The column should measure 6½" x 61½".

My Favorite Things Quilt Continued

SASHING AND BORDER STRIPS

1. Referring to the assembly diagram on page 19, sew together different lengths of 2"-wide cream print strips end to end interspersed with 2" colored squares until you have a strip that measures 2" x 61½". If you go over this measurement when assembling your strips, simply trim it to size. You will need a total of 23 of these strips. These are for the vertical inner sashing strips, side borders, and the top and bottom borders.

2. Referring to the assembly diagram, arrange the strips in sets of three, alternating them with the appliquéd columns. When you are satisfied with the arrangement, sew the sets of strips together. Reserve three of the 2" x 61½" strips for the top border and two of them for the bottom border.

COMPLETING THE QUILT

1. Referring to the assembly diagram on page 19, sew the sashing strips and side borders to the adjoining columns of appliquéd and pieced blocks.

2. Referring to the photo on page 11 for placement, back-stitch the words "My Favorite Things" with two strands of DMC 869 floss on the top border's middle strip. I used the Australian spelling of "Favourite" in my quilt.

3. Referring to the assembly diagram, sew 3 – 2" x 61½" cream print strips to create the top border. Then sew the border to the quilt top.

4. Referring to the assembly diagram, sew 2 – 2" x 61½" cream print strips to create the bottom border. Then sew the border to the bottom of the quilt.

5. Quilt, bind, and enjoy. My Favorite Things was professionally quilted with a flower vine motif along the cream print strips. The outline of the appliqué was also quilted.

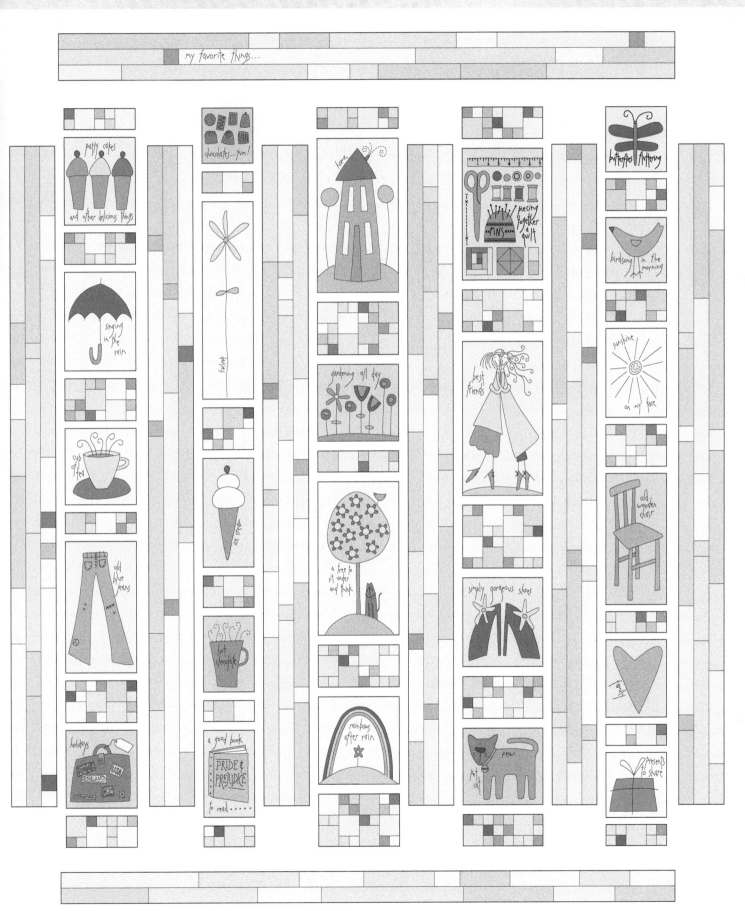

Assembly Diagram

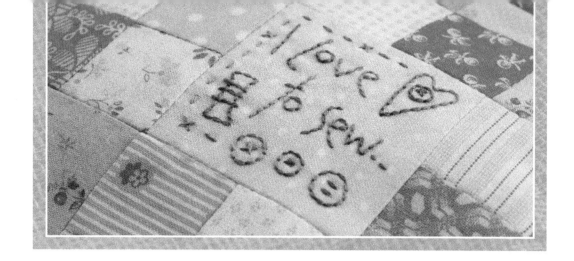

Sewing Case

Finished size: 5¾" x 9½" ◦ Designed and made by Anni Downs

If you're like me, it's hard to keep track of all those threads, pencils, scissors, needles, and other sewing necessities when on the go. Over the years, I tried different storage solutions but they never worked quite right. Thanks to my new saving grace—a sewing bag that I can take anywhere, I now have a place where I can easily store all of my current projects as well as my many sewing supplies.

FABRIC REQUIREMENTS

Bag front and back:
- 13 scraps of assorted colored prints
- 8 scraps of assorted cream/beige prints

Bag gusset and handles:
- 1 fat quarter linen

Lining:
- ⅓ yard lining fabric

- ¼ yard one-sided lightweight fusible fleece
- ¼ yard double-sided lightweight fusible fleece
- Weeks Dye Works 'Stone' floss
- 18" zipper
- 3⅜" x 9⅜" piece of template plastic

CUTTING INSTRUCTIONS

From linen, cut:
- 1 – 1½" x 19½" strip
- 1 – 3½" x 19½" strip
- 1 – 4" x 8¾" strip
- 2 – 2½" x 10½" strips

From assorted colored prints, cut:
- 32 – 1½" squares

From assorted cream/beige prints, cut:
- 32 – 1½" squares
- 14 – 2½" squares (Note that three of these squares have stitchery designs. All stitchery should be completed **before** the squares are trimmed to their exact size)

From lining fabric, cut:
- 2 – 6½" x 10½" rectangles
- 1 – 1⅛" x 19½" strip
- 1 – 3" x 19½" strip
- 1 – 4¼" x 10¼" rectangle

Sewing Case Continued

From one-sided fusible fleece, cut:
* 1 – 1½" x 19½" strip
* 1 – 3½" x 19½" strip

From double-sided fusible fleece, cut:
* 2 – 6½" x 10½" piece

From template plastic, cut:
* 1 – 3⅜" x 9⅜" piece

SEWING INSTRUCTIONS

1. Referring to the stitchery guide on page 104, backstitch the three designs for this project using two strands of the 'Stone' floss. Once complete, trim the stitchery blocks to 2½" square.

2. Sew together a 1½" colored print square and a 1½" cream print square. Repeat for all 64 squares.

3. Sew two of the units created in Step 2 to make a four-patch block. Repeat to make a total of 16 four-patch blocks.

4. Referring to the following diagram, sew together the four-patch blocks and 2½" squares. This piece should measure 6½" x 10½". Repeat this process for the back of the sewing case. Please note there are no stitchery panels on the back of the case.

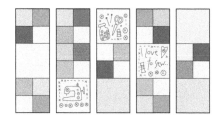

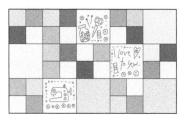

5. Place the lining (right side down), then the double-sided fusible fleece on top of that, and the pieced sewing case front (right side up) on top of that. Iron the three layers together. Repeat for the sewing case back.

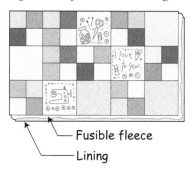

— Fusible fleece
— Lining

6. Using the sewing case template on page 104, cut out the sewing case front and back. The template includes a ¼" seam allowance.

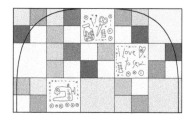

7. Iron the 1½" x 19½" one-sided fusible fleece strip to the wrong side of the 1½" x 19½" linen strip. Repeat for the 3½" x 19½" fusible fleece and linen strips.

8. Using a long machine basting stitch and a ½" seam allowance, join the two strips along the long sides. Press open.

½" seam allowance

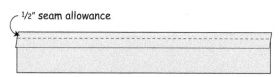

9. Centrally place the 18" zipper along the basted seam. Using a zipper foot, sew a ¼" out from each side of the closed zipper.

10. To create the gusset, sew the 4" x 8¾" linen strip to both ends of the zipper piece, forming a circle. Unpick the zipper basting line.

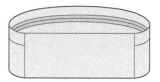

11. Mark the halfway points on the back and front case pieces and on the gusset.

12. Fold a 2½" x 10½" linen handle strip in half to measure 1¼" x 10½". Using a ¼" seam allowance, sew the long opening closed. Turn the strip right side out and press. Repeat once to create a second handle.

13. Position the handles centrally along the top of the case front and back pieces so their ends are 3½" apart and the ends are aligned with the raw edges of the case pieces. Baste in place.

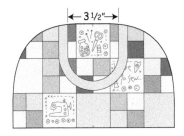

14. With right sides together, pin the base of the thin side of the gusset circle to the base of the case front piece, matching marked halfway points. Sew along the base of the case front, starting and stopping a ¼" from either end of the case front base. Clip the seam allowance of the gusset to the sewing line at the ¼" point.

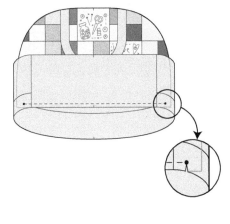

15. With right sides together, pin the base of the wide side of the gusset circle to the base of the case back piece, matching marked halfway points. Sew along the base of the case back, starting and stopping a ¼" from either end of the case back base. Clip the seam allowance of the gusset to the sewing line at the ¼" point.

16. Pin the remaining gusset length to each side of the case, matching up halfway points, and sew. Unzip the zipper and turn the case right side out.

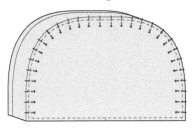

17. Fold and press the 1⅛" x 19½" lining strip under a ¼" along both long sides. Pin this to the inside top of the case gusset, covering all raw edges. Hand-stitch it in place. Repeat this for the 3" x 19½" lining strip, positioning it on the inside base of the gusset. Leave the ends unsewn as they will be covered by the lining base.

18. Using a glue stick, glue the seam allowance of the 4¼" x 10¼" lining fabric to the underside of the 3⅜" x 9⅜" template plastic piece. Position this in the base of the case. Then hand-stitch it in place, covering all raw edges as you sew.

19. Throw everything you need for your project in your new sewing case and have fun stitching!

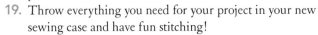

Needle Book

Finished size: 4" x 6" ◦ Designed and made by Anni Downs

I'm afraid my needle book collection is growing out of control, but I can't live without these great little organizers. The good thing about having such a large collection is that I can have one for every project I'm working on! This needle book has larger pockets that can easily accommodate embroidery thread and needle cards, and a multitude of other stitching supplies.

FABRIC REQUIREMENTS

Stitchery backgrounds:
- 7" x 10" piece of cream print

Patchwork cover:
- 9 scraps of assorted colored prints
- 7 scraps of assorted cream/beige prints

Lining:
- 1 fat eighth cream print

Inner pocket:
- 4 – 2½" x 3½" pieces of different blue prints
- 1 – 4" x 8½" piece of brown print for lining

Wool pin holder:
- 3½" x 5¼" piece of brown wool
- 3½" x 5¼" piece of blue wool

- ¼ yard lightweight fusible fleece
- Weeks Dye Works 'Stone' floss
- 11mm x 14mm oval shell button

CUTTING INSTRUCTIONS

From cream print, cut:
- ❊ 1 – 4½" x 6½" rectangle for stitchery background
- ❊ Heart template on page 105 for stitchery background
  (Note that both these pieces have stitchery designs. All stitchery should be completed **before** they are trimmed to their exact size.)

From assorted colored prints, cut:
- ❊ 16 – 1½" squares for patchwork cover

From assorted cream/beige prints, cut:
- ❊ 16 – 1½" squares for patchwork cover
- ❊ 4 – 2½" squares for patchwork cover

From blue prints, cut:
- ❊ 4 – 2½" x 3½" rectangles for inner pocket

From brown print, cut:
- ❊ 1 – 4" x 8½" rectangle for pocket lining

From cream print lining fabric, cut:
- ❊ 1 – 6½" x 12½" rectangle

From brown wool, cut:
* 1 – 3½" x 5¼" rectangle for wool pin holder

From blue wool, cut:
* 1 heart template on page 105 for wool pin holder

From fusible fleece, cut:
* 1 – 6½" x 12½" piece

SEWING INSTRUCTIONS

1. Referring to the stitchery guide on page 105, backstitch the two designs using two strands of Weeks Dye Works 'Stone' floss. Then trim the rectangular stitchery piece to 4½" x 6½" and the heart-shaped stitched piece to size **after** stitchery is complete.

2. Sew together a 1½" colored print square and a 1½" cream print square. Repeat for all 32 squares.

3. Sew two units created in Step 2 to make a total of 8 four-patch blocks.

4. Sew together the 4-patch blocks from Step 3 and the 2½" cream/beige print squares. The resulting unit should measure 6½" x 8½".

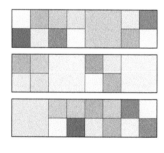

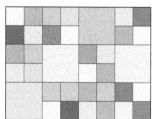

5. Appliqué the stitchery heart to the pieced section from Step 4, positioning it centrally on the right-hand side of the block.

6. Sew the 4½" x 6½" cream print stitchery block to the left of the pieced section from Step 4. This completes the front cover. It should measure 6½" x 12½".

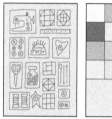

7. Iron the fusible fleece to the wrong side of the front cover.

8. Sew together the 4 – 2½" x 3½" blue print rectangles. The resulting unit should measure 3½" x 8½".

9. Sew the 4" x 8½" brown print pocket lining fabric to the top of the unit created in Step 8.

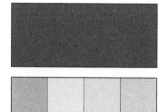

10. With right sides together, fold the unit from Step 9 in half and sew down the left side only. This creates the inner pocket.

11. Turn the inner pocket right side out, then align its base and left side with the raw edges of the 6½" x 12½" cream print lining fabric. Baste the pocket in place. Using two strands of Weeks Dye Works 'Stone' floss, sew a running stitch along the pocket's center seam allowance and its right side to create two pockets.

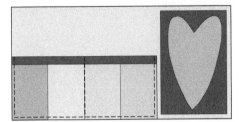

12. Referring to the previous diagram for placement, appliqué the blue wool heart centrally on the 3½" x 5¼" brown wool background. Pin this piece to the right side of the lining fabric and whipstitch it in place using two strands of the 'Stone' floss.

13. With right sides together, layer the backing cover on top of the front cover and sew around all sides, leaving a small opening for turning. Clip corners, turn right side out, and press.

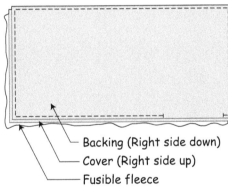

— Backing (Right side down)
— Cover (Right side up)
— Fusible fleece

14. Using three strands of the 'Stone' floss, make a button loop to the right of the rectangular stitchery panel. To make the loop, thread a loop through the fabric large enough to accommodate the button, plus a little more for good measure. Repeat this two more times to create a thick loop. With the same thread, use a blanket stitch and work around the loop, pulling it tight with each stitch.

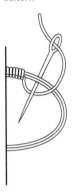

15. Attach a button to the right side of the needle book cover.

16. Fill the pockets with all your needle packets, scissors, and thread skeins and secure a few pins and needles to the woolen heart. Now you're ready to sew!

This needle book makes a handy home for needle packets and other sewing accessories.

Pincushion

Finished size: Approximately 2" x 3¼" • Designed and made by Anni Downs

As an avid pincushion collector, I have plenty of places to stash my pins but my favorite is one that I made several years ago. It is similar in shape to this pincushion and has been put to good use. After sticking far too many pins in it over the years, it certainly has seen better days. So I thought it was time to make a new one—this time, with some fun stitchery around the side.

FABRIC REQUIREMENTS
- 4" x 12" piece of linen
- 9 scraps of assorted cream and colored prints
- Weeks Dye Works 'Stone' floss
- Polyester fiberfill

CUTTING INSTRUCTIONS
From linen, cut:
✽ 1 – 2" x 10" rectangle for pincushion side (Note that this rectangle contains stitchery. The stitchery should be completed **before** the rectangle is trimmed to its exact size)

From assorted cream and colored prints, cut:
✽ 18 – 1½" squares for pincushion top and bottom

SEWING INSTRUCTIONS
1. Referring to the stitchery guide on page 106, backstitch the design for the pincushion side on the 4" x 12" linen rectangle using two strands of 'Stone' floss. Then trim the stitched piece to 2" x 10".
2. Sew together the 1½" assorted colored squares in rows of three to create a 9-patch block. Repeat for the remaining squares.

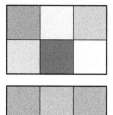

3. Trace the circle template on page 106 on the two 9-patch blocks and cut along this line. Note that the circle template includes a ¼" seam allowance.

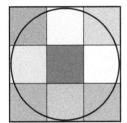

4. Sew together the 2" ends of the 2" x 10" stitched linen strip, leaving a 1" opening in the center for turning later.

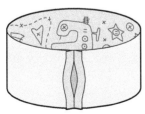

5. Heavily pin a 9-patch circle to the stitched linen strip, matching marked quarter points. Using a small machine stitch, sew together the pieces. Repeat this process for the remaining 9-patch circle.

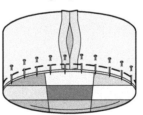

6. Turn the pincushion right side out. Stuff with polyester fiberfill, then slipstitch the opening closed. It is now ready for pins, pins, and more pins!

Snuggle Quilt

Finished size: 53¾" x 64¼" • Designed by Anni Downs
Made by Helen Vanderhel • Quilted by Belinda Betts

I truly love antique quilts, not just for their history but also for their warm colors and block designs. Many of them feature small and simple patchwork blocks that use a myriad of fabrics to create their designs. Several years ago, I designed this quilt using large blocks to spotlight all the wonderful large-scale prints available today. But for this book, I decided to downsize them and opted for a soft color palette that soothes the soul. This quilt is the perfect size to snuggle up in when you're relaxing at home.

FABRIC REQUIREMENTS

Blocks:
- 5 fat quarters or ⅓ yard each of assorted dusky pink prints
- 5 fat quarters or ⅓ yard each of assorted dusky blue/gray prints
- ¾ yard dark brown floral

Sashing:
- 1¼ yard cream toile
- Dark brown floral yardage listed under block yardage

Binding:
- ¾ yard dark brown floral

CUTTING INSTRUCTIONS

From each dusky pink print, cut:
❋ 12 – 5" squares for blocks

From each dusky blue/gray print, cut:
❋ 12 – 5" squares for blocks

From cream toile, cut:
❋ 8 – 5" strips the width of fabric for sashing. Then sub-cut these into 262 – 1¼" x 5" strips

From dark brown floral, cut:
❋ 19 – 1¼" strips the width of fabric for the blocks and sashing. Then sub-cut these into 623 – 1¼" squares
❋ 7 – 2½" strips the width of fabric for binding

Snuggle Quilt Continued

SEWING INSTRUCTIONS

1. With right sides together, layer a 1¼" dark brown floral square on top of one corner of a 5" dusky pink or dusky blue/gray print square. Then sew diagonally across the 1¼" dark brown floral square. Cut the corner, leaving a ¼" seam allowance. Then press the triangle open. Repeat this for all corners of the 120 dusky pink print and dusky blue/gray 5" squares.

2. Referring to the assembly diagram on page 33, arrange the 120 blocks in 12 rows of 10 blocks each.

3. Beginning with a 1¼" x 5" cream toile strip, sew together the 5" dusky pink print and dusky blue/gray print blocks in each row, alternating with a cream toile strip. End the row with a cream toile strip. Repeat 11 times to create of a total of 12 rows. Each row should measure 5" x 53¾".

4. Beginning with a 1¼" dark brown floral square, sew together 11 – 1¼" dark brown floral squares and 10 – 1¼" x 5" cream toile strips, alternating them. Repeat this 12 times to create a total of 13 rows. Each row should measure 1¼" x 53¾".

5. Referring to the assembly diagram on page 33, join the rows.

6. Quilt, bind, and enjoy.

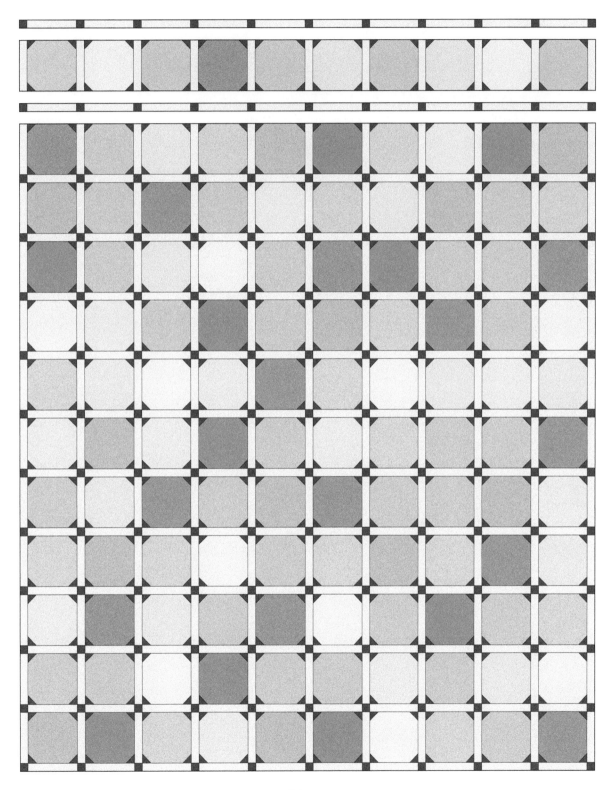

Assembly Diagram

Pillow

Finished size: 17" x 17" • Designed and made by Anni Downs

When it comes to creating an inviting home, pillows are a must. They represent hospitality, warmth, and comfort. A whimsical bird enlightens my patchwork pillow, while an array of wool blooms adds pizzazz.

FABRIC REQUIREMENTS

Appliqué block:
- 9" square of cream print
- Two scraps of blue prints for bird and wing (I used a different one for each)
- ¼" square of dark brown wool for bird eye
- Scrap of brown print for bird beak
- Bird eye center yardage listed in flower yardage

Flowers:
- 8" square of beige wool (this is also used for the bird eye center)
- 2½" square of dusky pink wool

Pillow patchwork:
- 12 scraps of assorted colored prints
- 8 – 10" squares of assorted cream prints

Inner border:
- 1 fat eighth or ⅛ yard brown print

Pillow back and lining:
- ¾ yards cream print (I used a cross-stitch design print)

- 1 yard lightweight fusible fleece
- DMC embroidery floss: Light brown (167), Brown (869), and Dark gray/brown (3021)
- 2¼ yards jumbo beige rick-rack
- 3 – 1"-wide buttons
- 3 snap fasteners or 3 circular Velcro closures
- 18" pillow form
- Template plastic

Pillow Continued

CUTTING INSTRUCTIONS

From cream print, cut:

❋ One 6½" square for the appliqué background (Please note this block contains appliqué and should be trimmed to size after the appliqué is completed)

From blue prints, cut:

❋ One bird template on page 100
❋ One bird wing template on page 100

From brown print, cut:

❋ One bird beak template on page 100

From beige wool, cut:

❋ Seven flower templates on page 107
❋ One bird eye center template on page 106

From dusky pink wool, cut:

❋ Seven flower center templates on page 107

From dark brown wool, cut:

❋ One bird eye template on page 106

From assorted colored prints, cut:

❋ 43 – 1½" squares for pillow patchwork
❋ 3 button tabs from the template on page 106
  (The tabs are cut **after** they are sewn)

From assorted cream/beige prints, cut:

❋ 31 – 1½" squares for pillow patchwork
❋ 64 – 2½" squares for pillow patchwork

From brown print, cut:

❋ 2 – 1" x 12½" strips for inner border
❋ 2 – 1" x 13½" strips for inner border

From cream print, cut:

❋ 1 – 17½" x 19" rectangle for pillow back
❋ 1 – 6½" x 17½" rectangle for pillow lining

From fusible fleece, cut:

❋ 1 – 17½" square
❋ 1 – 14" x 17½" rectangle
❋ 1 – 6½" x 17½" rectangle

From template plastic, cut:

❋ One button tab template on page 106

SEWING INSTRUCTIONS

1. Referring to the appliqué placement guide on page 100, appliqué the bird to the cream print background. Please note that you will need to add a ¼" seam allowance to the bird template if doing needle-turn appliqué. Do not add any seam allowance to the flowers. For the bird eye and center, place the cream wool bird eye center over the brown wool eye and secure it with a whipstitch. Using four strands of DMC 3021 floss, finish the eye with a French knot.

2. Referring to the stitchery guide on page 100, backstitch the wording with two strands of DMC Brown (869) floss and the bird legs with two strands of DMC Light brown (167) floss.

3. Set 23 – 1½" cream/beige squares and 23 – 1½" colored squares aside for the outer border and back of the pillow. Referring to the following diagram, sew together 6 – 1½" assorted colored squares and cream/beige squares. Repeat once to create a total of two rows. Then sew these two rows to the top and bottom of the appliqué block.

4. Referring to the previous diagram, sew together 8 – 1½" assorted colored squares and cream/beige squares. Repeat once to create a total of two rows. Then sew these rows to the sides of the appliqué block in the previous step.

5. Referring to the following diagram, sew together 4 – 2½" cream/beige squares. Repeat once to create a total of two rows. Then sew these rows to the top and bottom of the unit created in Step 4.

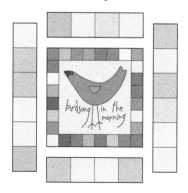

6. Referring to the previous diagram, sew together 6 – 2½" cream/beige squares. Repeat once to create a total of two rows. Then sew these rows to both sides of the unit created in Step 5.

7. Referring to the following diagram, sew 2 – 1" x 12½" brown print border strips to the top and bottom of the unit created in Step 6. Then sew 2 – 1" x 13½" brown print border strips to the sides of that unit.

8. Sew together a 1½" colored print square and a 1½" cream print square. Repeat to create a total of 23 two-patch units. Eight are for the front and 15 are for the back.

9. Sew together 6 – 2½" cream print squares. Referring to the following diagram, sew a two-patch unit from the previous step to one end of the strip of cream print squares. Repeat once to create a total of two rows. Then sew them to the top and bottom of the unit created in Step 8.

10. Referring to top left and bottom right units in the previous diagram, sew 6 two-patch units into sets of three to create a total of two 6-patch units.

11. Sew together 7 – 2½" cream print squares. Referring to the previous diagram, sew a 6-patch unit to one end of the cream print square strip. Repeat once to create a total of two rows. Then sew them to the sides of the unit created in Step 9.

12. Referring to the wool appliqué instructions on page 8 and photo on page 35 for appliqué placement, appliqué the beige wool flowers and dusky pink wool flower centers on the pillow front.

13. Iron the 17½" square fusible fleece to the wrong side of the pillow front.

14. To determine the amount of rick-rack you will need, place the rick-rick along the pillow top. Before cutting the rick-rack, make sure its "mountains" are placed evenly along each length. Then trim the edge of the rick-rack so the valley measures a generous ¼".

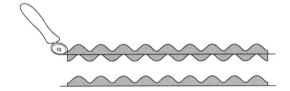

15. Pin the rick-rack along each edge of the pillow front and baste in place.

16. Using the remaining 15 two-patch units, make a total of 6 four-patch units. You will have 3 two-patch units left over.

17. Referring to the following diagram, sew together the 18 – 2½" cream print squares, 6 four-patch units, and 3 two-patch units into three rows. The more randomly the blocks are placed, the better they will look.

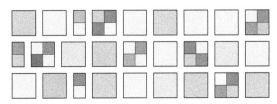

18. Join the three rows from Step 17. The resulting section should measure 6½" x 17½".

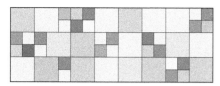

19. Iron the 6½" x 17½" fusible fleece to the back of the section created in Step 18.

20. For the button tab, fold the blue print scrap in half with right sides together. Using a wash-out pencil, trace the template on the blue print scrap. Using a small machine stitch, sew on the drawn line, leaving the straight edge open. Leaving about an ⅛" seam allowance, cut out the button tab. Turn right side out and press. Repeat twice to make a total of 3 button tabs.

21. Centering the button tabs 2¾" apart, baste them to the base of the 6½" x 17½" pieced pillow back.

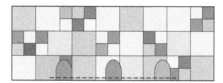

22. With right sides together, sew the base of the 6½" x 17½" pillow back lining to the base of the 6½" x 17½" pieced pillow back, sandwiching the tabs in between. Then turn right side up and press.

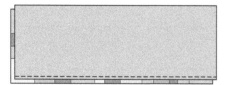

23. Iron the 14" x 17½" fusible fleece piece to the wrong side of the 17½" x 19" cream print pillow back piece, aligning the base and side seams. Then fold the top back down 2½". Fold it over another 2½" to disguise the raw edge. Then topstitch the folded edge in place.

Fold down 2 1/2"

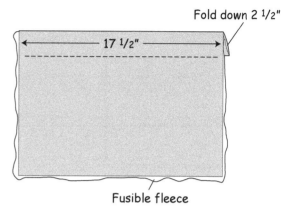

← 17 1/2" →

Fusible fleece

24. Lay the pieced pillow back over the cream print pillow back portion so the right sides face up. Measure the height and overlap the pieces so they measure 17½" from top to bottom. The overlap should be 2¾". Then baste the side seams together.

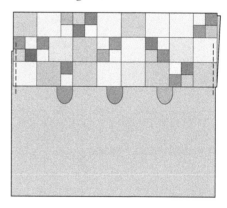

25. With right sides together, sew the pillow top to the pillow back. Finish the seam allowance with a zig-zag stitch or a similar stitch.

26. Turn the pillow right side out and sew snap fasteners or Velcro closures to the tabs and pillow base.

27. Attach a button to the top of each tab.

28. Insert the pillow form, then sit back and enjoy a good book!

A trio of button tabs enlivens
the back of this fanciful pillow.

Heat Bag

Finished size: 6" x 15" • Designed and made by Anni Downs

This whimsical project combines a gorgeous handkerchief linen that I happened upon one day and some wool that my husband hand dyed. Together, they make a calming heat bag, which works wonders for keeping your toes toasty warm or soothing weary shoulders after sewing all day. I even use one as a lap warmer on chilly days. To make the heat bag's cover easy to wash, I've included an inner bag filled with rice and fragrant lavender. You could also use wheat or barley as fillers.

FABRIC REQUIREMENTS

Appliqué background:
- 1 fat quarter or ¼ yard brown handkerchief linen

Wool appliqué:
- 4" square pieces of wool in gray/blue, caramel, beige, watermelon, and pea (I used various textures such as herringbone and plaid)

Patchwork section:
- Scraps of assorted cream and colored prints
- 3 – 15mm light brown buttons

Inner bag:
- ¼ yard cream homespun
- 3–4 cups long grain rice, wheat, or barley
- Optional: dried herbs such as lavender and essential oils for fragrance

- DMC Light gray/green embroidery floss (646)
- 1⅓ yards of ready-made ¼"-wide cream-colored piping

CUTTING INSTRUCTIONS

From brown handkerchief linen, cut:
* 1 – 6½" x 15½" rectangle
* 1 – 6½" x 14" rectangle
* 1 – 3½" x 6½" rectangle

From assorted cream and colored prints, cut:
* 18 – 1½" squares

From cream homespun, cut:
* 2 – 6½" x 15½" rectangles for inner bag

From assorted wool scraps, cut:
* Templates on page 107

SEWING INSTRUCTIONS

1. Referring to the guide above for placement, appliqué the wool flowers and leaves on the 6½" x 14" handkerchief linen background. **Before** appliquéing, note that 2¼" of the left-hand side should be blank as this section will be overlapped with the patchwork section later. Using three strands of DMC 646, backstitch the stems.

2. With right sides together, sew together 2 – 6½" x 15" cream homespun rectangles, leaving one of the short sides open. Turn right side out, then fill two-thirds full with rice, wheat, or barley. If you wish, add lavender or other dried herbs for fragrance. Then sew the opening closed. This completes the inner bag.

3. Sew three 1½" assorted colored and cream squares together to create a row. Repeat five times to create a total of 6 rows. Join the six rows. The resulting unit should measure 3½" x 6½".

4. Sew the 3½" x 6½" brown linen strip to one side of the unit created in Step 3. Press under. Set aside.

5. Turn the left side of the 6½" x 14" appliquéd linen block under a ½". Then turn it under again to hide the raw edge. Topstitch this folded end in place.

6. With right sides facing up, lay the patchwork section over the appliquéd linen block. Measure the width and overlap these two pieces so they total 15½" in width. The overlap should be 1¼". Then baste the top and bottom seams. This completes the heat bag front.

7. I purchased ready-made piping for my project. If you can't find suitable ready-made piping, you can create your own custom version using fine cording and fabric. Simply make a bias strip of fabric double the width of the cord, plus an extra ½" for the seam allowance. With wrong sides together, wrap the bias strip around the cord, and align the raw edges. Using a zipper foot on your sewing machine, baste the strip an ⅛" from the cord. This stitched line will be hidden once the cord is attached to the heat bag.

8. Aligning the raw edges of the piping and the bag front, pin the piping around the entire perimeter of the heat bag front. Clip the seam allowance of the piping at each corner to help it lay flat. Using the zipper foot on your sewing machine, sew the piping to the heat bag front.

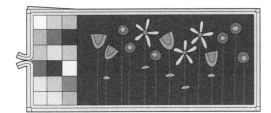

9. Start and finish by turning the piping ends outward, away from the heat bag. Then cut off excess fabric.

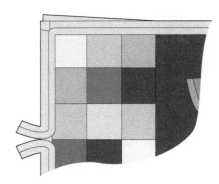

10. With right sides together, layer and pin together the heat bag front and back. Using a zipper foot on your sewing machine, sew around the perimeter. I finished off the seams with a zig-zag stitch.

11. Turn the heat bag right side out. Referring to the photo on pages 40-41, sew three buttons along the side of the patchwork section. Add Velcro tabs to the underside of the patchwork flap, and secure. Then insert the inner bag into the heat bag cover.

12. You can heat this bag in the microwave for about three minutes, depending on your microwave's strength. To avoid overheating, test your microwave in one-minute increments. Then sit back and enjoy the warmth!

Daisy Quilt

Finished size: 60½" x 70½" • Designed and made by Anni Downs • Quilted by Belinda Betts

Daisies are my favorite flowers. I love them for their softness and long-lasting blooms. They last forever in my garden as well as in a vase.

FABRIC REQUIREMENTS

Appliqué background:
- 1 yard light cream print

Appliqué pieces:
- ¼ yard pale blue/gray print for petals
- ⅛ yard green stripe for leaves
- Scraps of yellow print for flower centers

Patchwork strips:
- 17 fat quarters or ⅓ yard each of assorted cream, caramel, and blue prints

Binding:
- ¾ yard brown print

- DMC green (3011) embroidery floss

CUTTING INSTRUCTIONS

From light cream print, cut:
- ❊ 8 – 5½" x 18½" rectangles (All appliqué blocks should be completed **before** they are trimmed to their exact size)

From assorted cream, caramel, and blue prints, cut:
- ❊ 85 – 3" x 18½" strips (five from each of the 17 assorted prints)

From light blue/gray print, cut:
- ❊ 8 petal templates on page 84

From green print, cut:
- ❊ 8 leaf templates on page 84

From yellow print, cut:
- ❊ 8 flower center templates on page 84

From brown print, cut:
- ❊ 7 – 2½" strips the width of fabric for binding

SEWING INSTRUCTIONS

1. Referring to the appliqué placement guide on page 84, appliqué the daisy petals, centers, and leaves to the 8 – 5½" x 18½" cream print background blocks.
2. Referring to the appliqué placement guide on page 84, backstitch the stems using three strands of DMC green (3011) embroidery floss.
3. Sew the 85 – 3" x 18" cream, caramel, and blue print strips end to end to create 8 – 3" x 70½" strips. Continue sewing the strips end to end.

4. Cut two of each of the strip measurements listed in the assembly diagram on page 47. Make sure the fabrics in the two cuts of each length differ from one another and avoid placing two of the same fabrics side by side. Referring to the assembly diagram, arrange the strips and appliqué blocks.
5. Sew together the pairs of strips that are the same lengths.

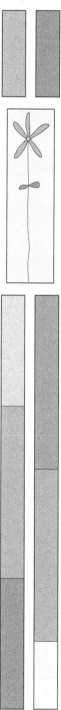

6. Press the pieced strips from Step 5. Referring to the assembly diagram, sew them to the top and bottom of the daisy blocks.

7. Referring to the assembly diagram, sew the remaining strips between the units created in Step 6.

8. Quilt, bind, and enjoy. I had my quilt professionally done using an all-over design of daisies.

Assembly Diagram

Punchneedle Door Hanger

Finished size: 4¼" x 5½" • Designed and made by Anni Downs

I am obsessed with punchneedle. I love the texture of this ancient art form and the way it allows me to mix threads to achieve subtle variations in color such as blending leaves into a tree. It's like painting with thread!

FABRIC REQUIREMENTS

- 8" square weavers cloth
- 1 fat eighth or ¼ yard beige star print
- 4" x 5" piece of gray/teal herringbone wool
- DMC embroidery floss: Ecru, Light teal (524), Yellow (729), Light champagne (738), Dark champagne (739), Brown (869), Blue (926), Light green (3012), Purple (3041), Medium green (3348), Raspberry (3721), and Orange (3776)
- ¼ yard heavyweight iron-on interfacing
- Punchneedle tool
- Small interlocking embroidery hoop
- Assorted 6mm–11mm buttons
- 10 inches thin rusty wire

CUTTING INSTRUCTIONS

From beige star print, cut:
❊ 2 – 5" x 6½" rectangles for backing

From interfacing, cut:
❊ 2 – 5" x 6½" rectangles

SEWING INSTRUCTIONS

1. Using a light source and Pigma pen, trace the design on page 77 on weavers cloth. Place the weavers cloth in the embroidery hoop and stretch until taut.
2. Using the instructions that accompanied your punchneedle tool and following the stitchery color guide on page 50, stitch the design.
3. When you have finished punching, use your needle to move any loops and sharpen distorted lines. Clip any loose ends on the front of the design back to the height of the loops. Steam press the design, then cut out the weavers cloth about a ½" away from the edge of the punchneedle design.
4. Turn under the seam allowance of the punchneedle and press it into position with a hot iron.

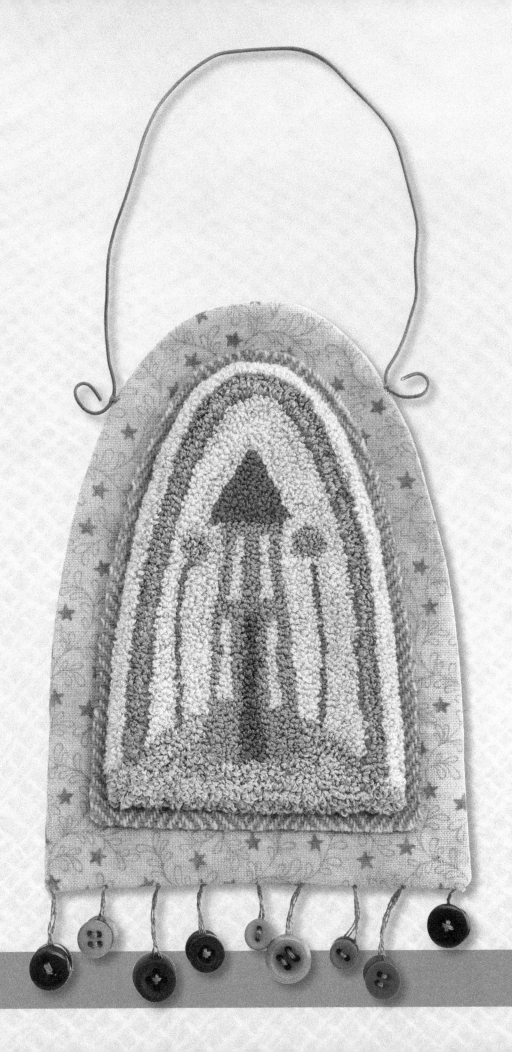

STITCHERY COLOR GUIDE

The DMC floss colors below are listed in the order in which they should be stitched. All items should be stitched with three strands:

- Roof: 3721
- Windows: 739
- Door and tree trunks: 869
- House walls: 926
- Grass and tree foliage: 3012 (2 strands) and 3348 (1 strand) (Combine these three strands in the needle)
- Outer rainbow line: 3041 (All other rainbow lines should be stitched side by side as closely as possible in the following order: 926, 3012, 729, 3776, and 3721)
- Background: Ecru, 738, and 739 (I used a different color or a combination of colors every time I rethreaded the needle)
- Background highlight: 524 (Use this sparingly to add a hint of color. This can be applied once the background is complete)

5. Centrally position the punchneedle on the wool and slipstitch it into place using a matching thread. Then cut out the wool about a ¼" from the edge of the punchneedle design.

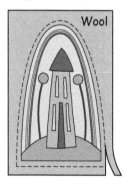

6. Iron the interfacing to the back of the 2 – 5" x 6½" beige star print backing pieces. Trace the punchneedle backing template on page 77 on the wrong side of one of these pieces. With right sides together, sew on the drawn line, leaving a small opening at the base for turning.

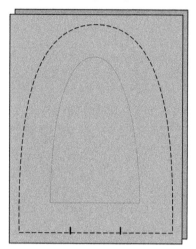

7. Trim an ⅛" seam allowance and clip corners. Turn right side out and press. If you wish, insert a few cloves or lavender for fragrance and sew the opening closed.

8. Slipstitch the wool to the beige star print backing.

9. Referring to the photo on page 49, attach buttons to the base of the punchneedle piece every half inch. To do this, first secure the thread to the backing, then thread it through the back of a button to the top and bring the thread through another hole to the back. Select a second button and bring the thread from the back of this button to the front. Bring the thread to the back of the second button, then bring the thread to the backing fabric and finish off. Repeat this for each button. Sandwiching the thread between two buttons makes the buttons sit perfectly.

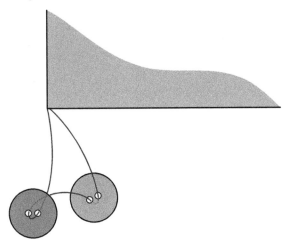

10. Bend the 10" length of wire until you are satisfied with the shape. Referring to the photo on page 49 for placement, hand-stitch the wire to the punchneedle. Then hang on a doorknob or hook.

Table Runner

Finished size: 12" x 30" • Designed and made by Anni Downs

I love having friends over to chat. Of course, we inevitably end up indulging in a cup of tea, coffee, or hot chocolate (my favorite!) and a sugary sweet treat. You can customize this table runner to fit your tabletop. For a fun twist, adapt the design into complementary placemats or coasters.

FABRIC REQUIREMENTS

Appliqué backgrounds:

- 1 fat eighth or 1/8 yard cream dot

Patchwork blocks:

- 8 – 10" squares of assorted cream/beige prints
- 8 – 10" squares of assorted colored prints

Appliqué pieces:

- Scraps of assorted colored prints

Backing:

- 1/2 yard cream print

- 1/2 yard lightweight fusible fleece
- DMC embroidery floss: Light brown (167), Blue (926), and Raspberry (3721)
- 28 inches jumbo rick-rack

CUTTING INSTRUCTIONS

From cream dot, cut:

- 9 – 3½" squares for appliqué backgrounds

From cream print, cut:

- 1 – 12½" x 30½" rectangle for backing

From assorted cream/beige prints, cut:

- 32 – 2½" squares for patchwork blocks (4 squares from each fabric)
- 75 – 1½" squares for patchwork blocks (10 squares from each fabric)

From assorted colored prints, cut:

- 76 – 1½" squares for patchwork blocks (10 squares from each fabric)
- 3 of each template on page 105 for appliqué pieces

From fusible fleece, cut:

- 1 – 12½" x 30½" piece

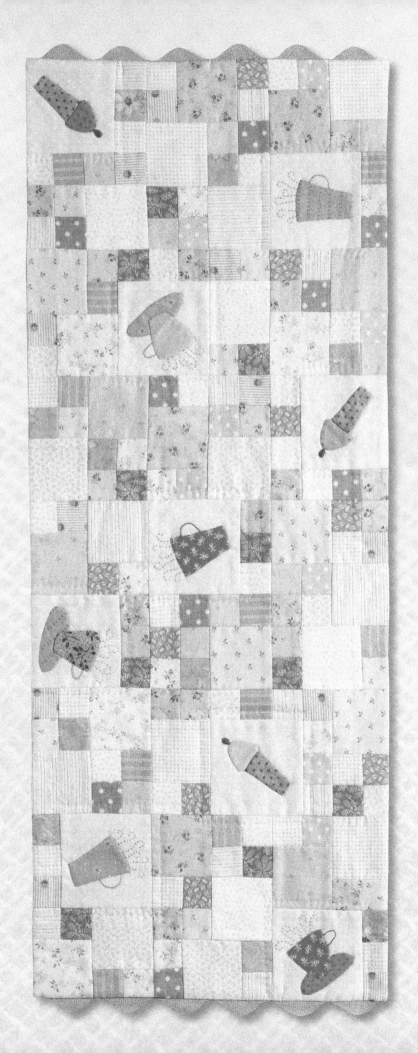

Table Runner Continued

SEWING INSTRUCTIONS

The table runner top is made of three different blocks (A, B, and C). I pieced the top **before** appliquéing the necessary blocks.

Block A

1. Sew a 1½" colored print square to each side of a 1½" cream/beige square. Then sew this unit to one side of a 3½" cream dot square.

2. Sew together a 1½" colored print square and a 1½" cream/beige print square. Then sew this unit to one side of a 2½" cream print square. Repeat to create a total of two units.

3. Referring to the following diagram, join the three units from Steps 1 and 2 to create Block A. The block should measure 4½" x 6½". Repeat Steps 1–3 to make a total of 5 Block As.

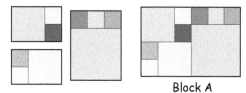

Block A

Block B

1. Sew a 1½" cream/beige print square to each side of a 1½" colored print square. Then sew this unit to one side of a 3½" cream dot square.

2. Sew a 1½" cream/beige print square to a 1½" colored print square to create a two-patch unit. Repeat to make a total of 4 two-patch units.

3. Sew together 2 two-patch units to create a four-patch unit. Then sew this unit to one side of a 2½" cream print square.

4. Sew together the remaining two-patch units end to end.

5. Sew the unit from Step 4 to the right of the unit from Step 1 and to the left of the unit from Step 3 to create Block B. The block should measure 4½" x 6½". Repeat Steps 1–5 to make a total of 4 Block Bs.

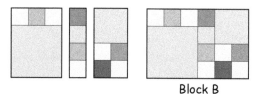

Block B

Block C

1. Sew together a 1½" cream/beige square and 1½" colored print square to create a two-patch unit. Repeat to make a total of 6 two-patch units.

2. Sew together 2 two-patch units to create a four-patch unit. Then sew a four-patch unit to a 2½" cream print square. Repeat to create a total of 2 units.

3. Sew the two units from Step 2 together.

4. Sew a two-patch unit to each side of a 2½" cream/beige print square.

5. Sew the unit from Step 4 to the left of the unit from Step 3 to create Block C. The block should measure 4½" x 6½". Repeat Steps 1–5 to make a total of 6 Block Cs.

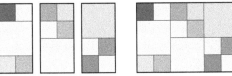

Block C

ASSEMBLING THE TOP

1. Referring to the following diagram, arrange the 5 Block As, 4 Block Bs, and 6 Block Cs. Note that some of the blocks will need to be placed upside down. Sew the blocks together.

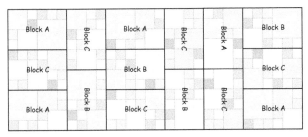

2. Referring to the following diagram, appliqué the three Tea Cup blocks, three Cupcake blocks, and three Mug blocks to the 9 cream dot appliqué background blocks. Using two strands of DMC 3721 floss, satin-stitch a cherry to the top of each cupcake. Backstitch the Mug and Tea Cup handles with two strands of floss that match the Tea Cup and Mug fabrics. Using two strands of DMC 167 embroidery floss, sew a running stitch for the steam lines on the Tea Cup and Mug appliqué blocks.

3. Iron the fusible fleece to the wrong side of the table runner top.
4. Place the rick-rack on the sides of the table runner top. Then cut two strips of it to size, making sure the "mountains" are placed evenly along each side before cutting.
5. Trim the edge of the rick-rack so the valley measures a generous ¼".

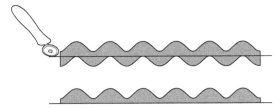

6. Pin the two strips of rick-rack along each side of the table runner top and baste them in place.

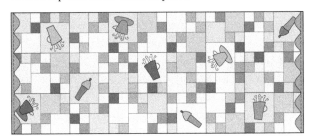

7. With right sides together, pin the 12½" x 30½" cream print backing to the table runner top. Then sew around all four sides, leaving a small opening along one side for turning. Clip the corners, then turn right side out. Press. Sew the opening closed.
8. Quilt the table runner. I used a simple design, quilting a ¼" out from each appliqué block. Now you're ready to invite friends over for a chat while sharing a cupcake and a cup of tea!

Bag

Finished size: 10" x 12" • Designed and made by Anni Downs

My countless bags are the colors of the rainbow, which often makes it hard to find one that matches what I am wearing. So I decided to make one that would go with most of my wardrobe. Because I love the look and texture of natural fibers, I chose linen for mine. The bag's back has a small opening that makes it easy to widen the top in case you can't find your keys!

FABRIC REQUIREMENTS
Bag front and back:
* ¾ yard linen

Lining:
* ½ yard blue floral

Binding:
* ⅛ yard solid brown

* ½ yard lightweight fusible fleece
* Valdani perle 8 thread in brown/purple (0545)
* DMC blue (3768) embroidery floss
* 11mm x 14mm oval button

CUTTING INSTRUCTIONS
From linen, cut:
* 2 – 3½" x 22½" strips for handles
* 1 – 3½" x 30" strip for gusset
* 2 – 12" x 14" rectangles for bag front and bag back

From lining fabric, cut:
* 1 – 3½" x 30" strip for gusset
* 4 – 2" x 3½" rectangles for handle base covers
* 2 – 12" x 14" rectangles for bag front and back

From brown solid, cut:
* 1 – 2¼" x 26" strip for binding
* 2 – 1" x 22½" strips for handles

From fusible fleece, cut:
* 2 – 12" x 14" pieces
* 1 – 3½" x 30" strip

From template plastic, cut:
* 1 main bag template on pages 108-109
* 1 gusset template on page 110

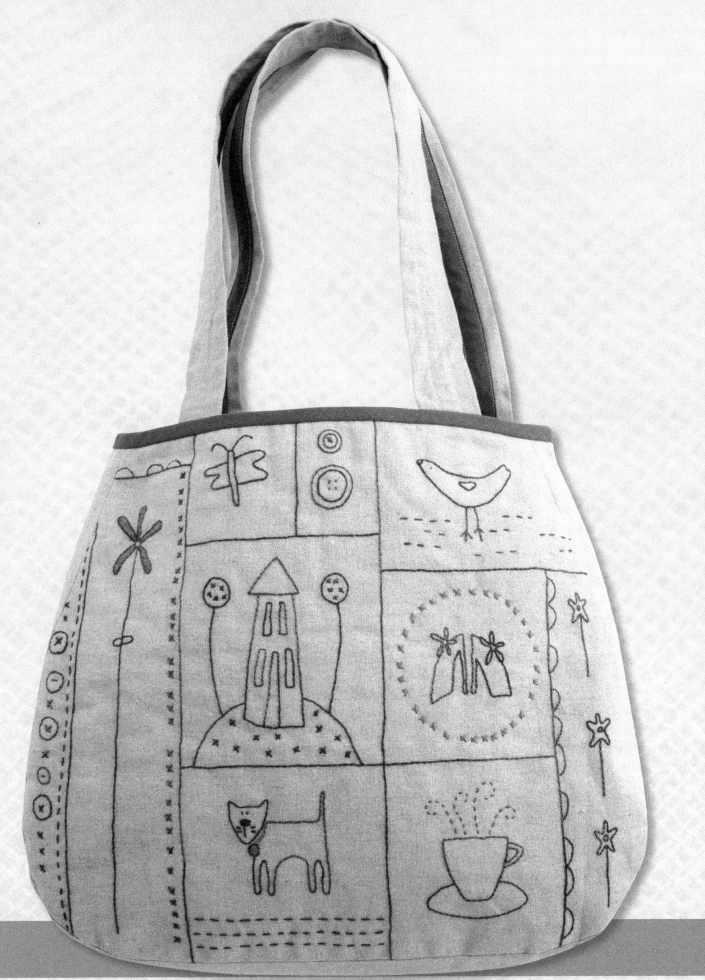

Bag Continued

SEWING INSTRUCTIONS

1. Referring to the stitchery guide on pages 108–109, trace the stitchery images on a 12" x 14" linen piece. Then stitch the design elements using a backstitch **except** where there are Xs (which are cross stitched), a dashed line (which are done with a running stitch), and the fill of the daisy petals and the nameplate on the cat collar (which are satin-stitched). Use the Valdani dark brown thread and backstitch for everything **except** the crosses around the shoes and cat collar, which are stitched with 3 strands of DMC blue (3768) embroidery floss (the fill of the name plate on the cat collar and the daisy petals use just one strand of DMC 3768).

2. Press the stitched bag front. Iron the fusible fleece to the wrong side of the bag front. Repeat for the bag back. Place the bag front/back template over the stitched bag front and trace its shape, then cut on the traced line. Repeat for the 12" x 14" bag back piece. Use the same template to cut the front and back lining bag pieces, using the 2 – 12" x 14" blue floral lining rectangles.

3. Iron the 3½" x 30" piece of fusible fleece to the wrong side of the linen gusset strip. Place the thin end of the gusset template on page 110 at one end of the strip and trace the two curved sides on to the gusset strip. Then cut on the drawn line. Repeat for the other end of the gusset strip. Repeat this process for the lining.

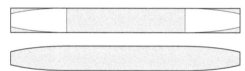

4. Mark the halfway points on the gusset strip and on the bag front and back pieces.

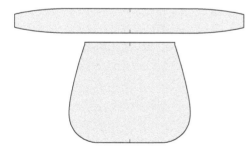

5. With right sides together, pin one side of the gusset to the bag front, matching up the marked points. Then sew the gusset to the bag front. Repeat for the bag back.

6. Repeat Steps 4–5 for the bag lining.

7. With right sides together, fold a 3½" x 22½" handle strip in half so it measures 1¾" x 22½". Sew along the long open edge. Then turn right side out and press so the seam allowance is in the center. Repeat for the second handle strip.

8. Fold the long sides of a 1" x 22½" solid brown strip in a quarter inch on both sides. Pin this strip centrally to one handle length, covering the seam line. Topstitch each edge of the brown strip in place. Repeat for the second solid brown strip.

9. Pin the handles to the right side of the bag lining so their ends are 1½" from the top edge of the bag lining and they are 4½" apart from each other. The solid brown strips should sit on the underside of the handle.

10. Fold a 2" x 3½" handle base cover strip in half to measure 2" x 1¾". With right sides together, sew around all three open sides, leaving a small opening along one side for turning. Clip corners, turn right side out, and press. Repeat to make a total of 4 of these units.

11. Place the units from Step 10 over the base of the bag handles so they sit a ½" from the top edge of the bag. Sew around all four sides of each tab, securing the handles in place.

12. To make the bag back opening, mark the center point on the back top edge of the blue floral lining. Using a Pigma pen, draw a line 3" down from this mark on the wrong side of the fabric.

13. With right sides together, nestle the linen inside the lining. Be sure the back of the linen bag is facing the back of the blue floral lining. Pin the linen and lining in place. Sew an ⅛" from the drawn line. Cut on the drawn line and clip into the corners. Turn right side out and press.

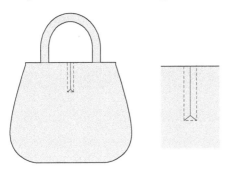

14. Machine baste the top edge of the bag, being careful not to sew over the bag handles.

15. With wrong sides together, press the 2¼" x 26" solid brown strip in half lengthwise. With right sides together and raw edges even, layer the solid brown strip on the top of the bag front. Begin and end the binding at the back opening, tucking its raw edges under at each end. The cutting measurements give you more binding than necessary so you can cut it to fit at this stage.

16. Roll the folded edge of the binding strip over to the lining and hand-stitch along the previous sewing line, covering the line of machine stitches.

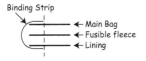

Binding Strip
← Main Bag
← Fusible fleece
← Lining

17. To make a button loop, make a loop at the top of the bag opening by threading Valdani perle 8 (0545) thread through the fabric, making sure the loop is large enough to accommodate the button. Repeat this two more times to create a thicker loop. With the same thread, use a blanket stitch to work around the loop, pulling it tight with each stitch.

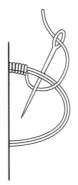

18. Attach a button to the opposite fabric side of the loop.

19. Fill your bag and go shopping for some scrumptious clothes and shoes!

Coin Purse

Finished size: 4" x 5" ❖ Designed and made by Anni Downs

My husband tends to leave all his loose change lying around everywhere. I have found a way to work this situation to my advantage by claiming any loose change for my coin purse! When I have enough saved up, I think I'll go buy a new pair of shoes!

FABRIC REQUIREMENTS
- 1 fat eighth or ¼ yard linen
- 1 fat eighth or ¼ yard blue floral for lining
- DMC embroidery floss: Putty (646) and Blue (3768)
- 5" beige zipper

CUTTING INSTRUCTIONS
From linen, cut:
❋ 2 templates on page 111 (Note that one piece has stitchery and all stitchery should be completed **before** it is trimmed to its exact size)

From lining fabric, cut:
❋ 2 templates on page 111

SEWING INSTRUCTIONS
1. Referring to the stitchery guide on page 111, trace the words and shoe image on the linen with a fine Pigma pen. Using two strands of DMC 3768 floss, backstitch the shoes, shoe circle, and cross border. Using two strands of DMC 3768 floss, satin-stitch the flowers on the shoes. Using two strands of DMC 646, backstitch the words. Then press.

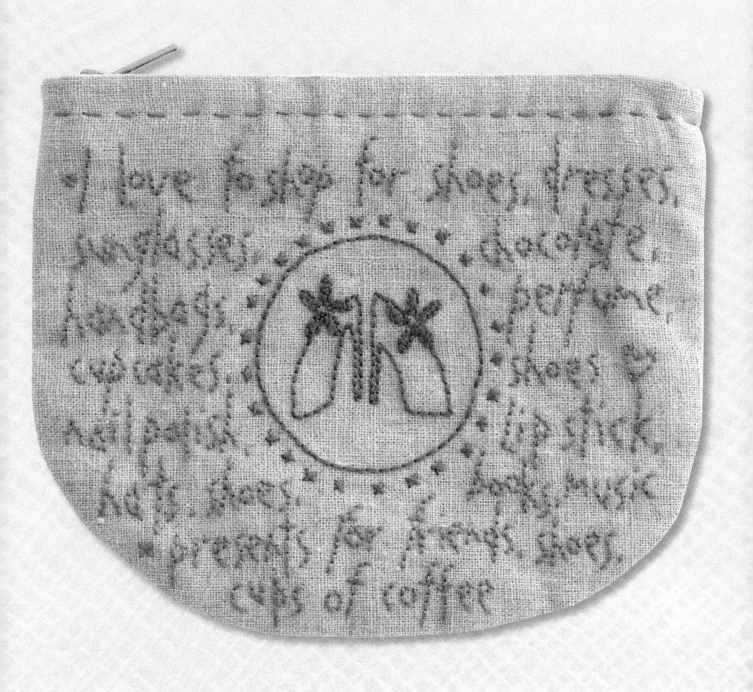

2. With right sides together, sew together the two linen pieces along the curved edge. Turn right side out.

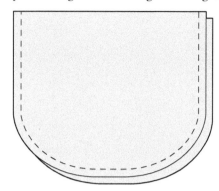

3. Fold the top edge under ¾" and press. Using a pencil, lightly mark a ¼" down on the right side of the linen.

4. Pin the closed zipper along one top side of the linen so the teeth are just hidden by the edge. Using a small running stitch and two strands of DMC 646, stitch the zipper to the edge of the linen along the drawn line on one edge only.

5. Open the zipper. Pin the open zipper along the remaining side of the purse and sew the second side as directed in Step 4. Before stitching, make sure the zipper is aligned with the first side.

6. With right sides together, sew together the two lining pieces along the curved edge.

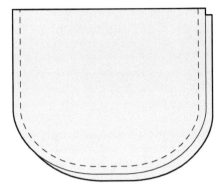

7. Fold the top edge of the lining under a ¼". With wrong sides together, nestle the lining within the linen enclosure and pin it an ⅛" below the zipper teeth. Slipstitch the lining to the zipper to hide all raw edges. Be sure to fold the zipper ends down so they will be encased in the lining. To make it easier to sew, I turn my purse inside out when sewing the lining where the zipper meets.

Travel Document Holder

Finished size: 4½" x 9½" • Designed and made by Anni Downs

One of my favorite things is traveling to fun places. For the longest time I had a boring fluorescent orange document holder for my passports, tickets, and boarding passes but this new organizer is so much more me. It has pockets for everything, including the all-important pen! This project could also easily double as a checkbook holder.

FABRIC REQUIREMENTS

Travel holder front:
- 1 fat quarter linen
- 9 scraps of assorted colored prints
- 5" square of cream print (If you use a hoop to stitch, you will need more)

Lining:
- 1 fat quarter blue floral

Inner pockets:
- 1 fat eighth cream floral

- ½ yard heavyweight iron-on interfacing
- Weeks Dye Works 'Stone' floss
- 2 small magnetic closures

CUTTING INSTRUCTIONS

From linen, cut:
- ❊ 1 – 8" x 10" rectangle
- ❊ 2 – 3¼" x 10" rectangles
- ❊ 2 – 1½" x 3" rectangles
- ❊ 1 – 2½" x 6¼" rectangle

From assorted colored prints, cut:
- ❊ 14 – 1½" squares
- ❊ 4 – 1½" x 1¾" rectangles

From blue floral, cut:
- ❊ 1 – 10" x 15½" rectangle

From cream floral, cut:
- ❊ 1 – 5" x 6½" rectangle
- ❊ 1 – 5" x 3¼" rectangle

From interfacing, cut:
- ❊ 2 – 10" x 15½" pieces

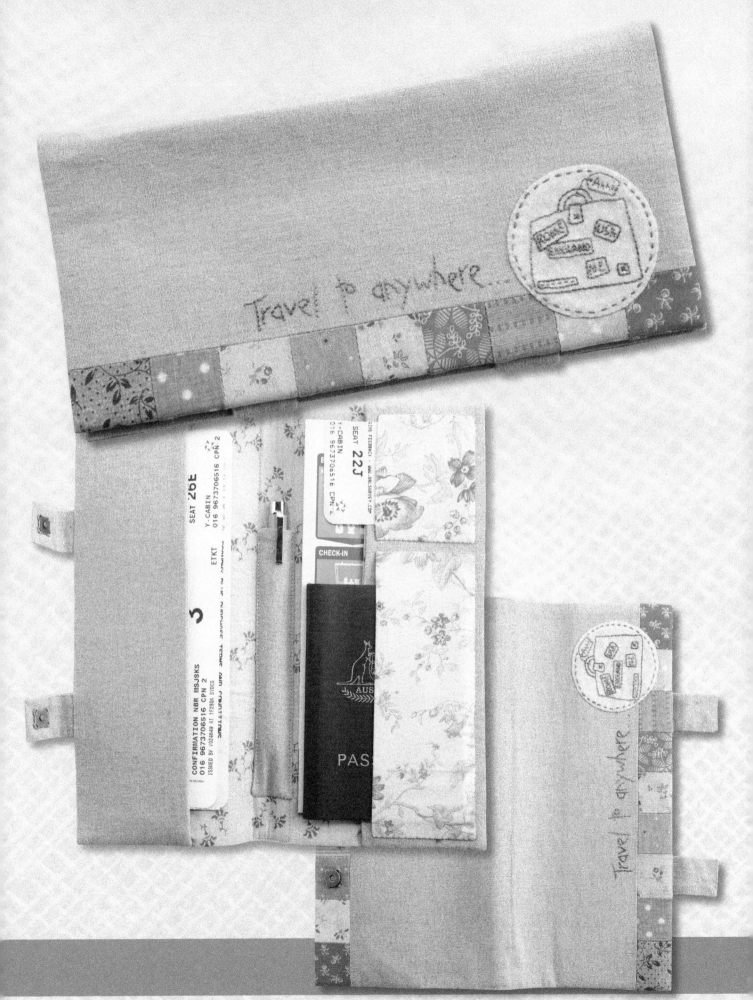

SEWING INSTRUCTIONS

1. Sew together 7 – 1½" assorted colored print squares side by side. Sew a 1½" x 1¾" colored print piece to each end of the row of squares just pieced. Repeat to create a total of two pieced 1½" x 10" strips.

2. Sew the pieced strips created in Step 1 to each 10" side of the 8" x 10" linen rectangle.

3. Referring to the stitchery guide on page 77, trace the design on the cream print background. Using two strands of 'Stone' thread, backstitch the suitcase circle. Then appliqué the cream print stitched circle to the linen cover about ¾" from the base and right raw edge.

4. Referring to the photo on page 65 for placement, trace, then backstitch the words "Travel to anywhere…" with two strands of 'Stone' thread.

5. With right sides together, fold a 1½" x 3" linen button flap so it measures 1½" square. Sew along the sides, then turn right side out. Repeat once.

6. Baste the button flaps to the base of the cover 2½" from either side of the cover.

7. With right sides together, sew the 3¼" x 10" linen pocket strips to the cover, sandwiching the button flaps in-between. Press open.

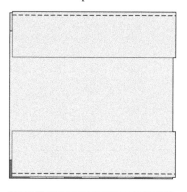

8. Iron one 10" x 15½" interfacing piece to the wrong side of the cover and one to the wrong side of the 10" x 15½" blue floral lining.

9. With right sides together, sew the lining to the cover, leaving a 3" opening along one side for turning. Clip corners, turn right side out, and press. This is difficult to do, so be persistent!

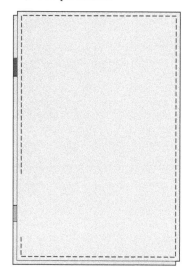

10. Fold the pocket strips back to the edge of the pieced row of squares. Using a matching thread, whipstitch along the sides to create the pockets.

11. Fold the 2½ "x 6¼" linen strip in half so it measures 1¼" x 6¼". Then sew around all three open sides, leaving a small opening along one side for turning. Clip corners, turn right side out, and press. This is the pen pocket.

12. Pin the pen pocket to the center of the blue floral lining 1" from the left side. Stitching from one side of the document holder to the other, sew the sides of the pen pocket in place, just catching them as you go.

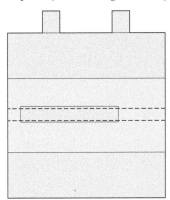

13. With right sides together, fold the 5" x 6½" cream floral inner pocket in half so it measures 2½" x 6½". Then sew around all three open sides, leaving a small opening on one side for turning. Clip corners, turn right side out, and press.

14. Pin the pocket created in Step 13 to the linen pocket a ¼" from the left edge of the document holder. Slipstitch the cream floral pocket to the linen background.

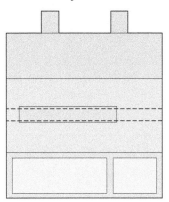

15. Repeat steps 13 and 14 for the second 5" x 3¼" cream floral inner pocket. When folded, it should measure 2½" x 3¼". Position it a ¼" from the right edge of the document holder before slipstitching it in place.

16. Sew the magnetic closures to the flap and back of the document holder along the pieced row of squares.

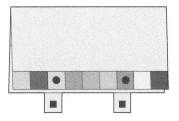

17. Fill your new document holder with your passport and tickets to somewhere fabulous!

Shoe Bag & Shoe Stuffers

Shoe Bag finished size: 12" x 15¾" • Designed and made by Anni Downs
Shoe Stuffers finished size: Approximately 3" x 6½" • Designed and made by Anni Downs

Shoes, glorious shoes. We can never have too many, can we? If you're like me, they are a bit of an obsession. What better way to keep them safe while traveling than with this handy cloth bag! I made some of these handy shoe accessories years ago and still use them today. And to help your shoes hold their shape, try these easy-to-make inserts. To keep your shoes smelling fresh, add dried lavender to the shoe stuffer contents.

SHOE BAG FABRIC REQUIREMENTS

Bag body:
* ½ yard light blue print

Appliqué background:
* 7" square of cream stripe

Appliqué pieces:
* 4" x 6" scrap of raspberry print for shoes
* 2½" x 5" scrap of blue print for flowers
* 1" x 2" scrap of yellow print for flower centers

Patchwork strips:
* Scraps of assorted colored prints

* 1¾ yards of ¼" cording or 9mm ribbon

SHOE BAG CUTTING INSTRUCTIONS

From light blue print, cut:
❊ 2 – 12½" x 15½" rectangles for bag body
❊ 2 – 3" x 12½" rectangles for bag body

From cream stripe, cut:
❊ 1 template from page 112 for the appliqué background
   (You will need to add a ¼" seam allowance to the template)

From raspberry print, blue print, and yellow print scraps, cut:
❊ 2 shoe templates on page 112
❊ 2 flower templates on page 112
❊ 2 flower center templates on page 112

From assorted colored prints, cut:
❊ 24 – 1½" squares for patchwork strips

From cord or ribbon, cut:
❊ 2 – 28"-long pieces

SHOE BAG SEWING INSTRUCTIONS

1. Referring to the appliqué placement guide on page 112, appliqué the templates to the 7" cream stripe background piece.

2. Appliqué the unit created in Step 1 to one 12½" x 15½" light blue print bag body piece 3 inches from the bottom.

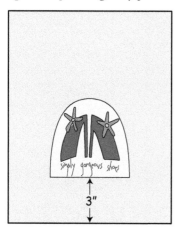

3. Sew together 12 – 1½" colored print squares end to end. Repeat to create another row of pieced squares. Then sew the two rows to the top of the 2 – 12½" x 15½" light blue print bag body pieces.

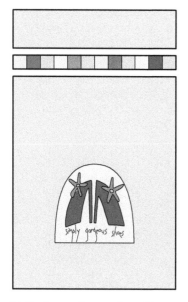

4. Referring to the previous diagram, sew the 2 – 3" x 12½" rectangles to the top of the two units created in Step 3.

5. Using a wash-out pencil, draw a line ¾" down from the seam of the pieced strip of squares for the casing. Then draw another line ⅝" below the first line.

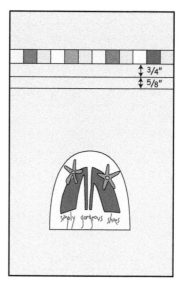

6. With right sides together, sew the bag front to the bag back along the bottom and side seams, leaving an opening between the drawn casing lines.

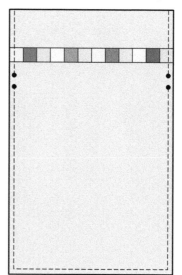

7. To make the bottom of the bag flat, match the base seam to the side seam, right sides together, so that the sewn corner of the bag forms a point. Then measure 1¼" from the point along the center seam. Draw a line at this point perpendicular to the seam and sew on the drawn line, which should be 2½" in length. Turn the bag right side out.

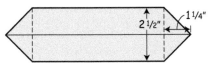

8. Press the top of the bag under a ½", then press the light blue strip under to the edge of the patchwork strip's seam. Pin this in place.

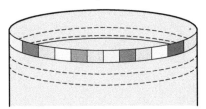

9. Sew on the drawn lines to form a casing for the cording.

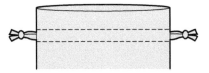

10. Attach a safety pin to one end of the cording and thread it through one opening of the casing all the way around, then back out through the same opening. Then tie the ends together. Repeat with the other length of cording, pulling it through the opposite casing opening. Pull both cords to close the bag.

SHOE STUFFERS FABRIC REQUIREMENTS

Main body fabric:
- 1 fat eighth blue and cream check

Fabric bands:
- 4" square of blue print

Button covers:
- 3" square of raspberry print

Patchwork strips:
- Scraps of assorted colored prints

- Cover button kit for ½" buttons
  (You will need 2 buttons)
- Polyester fiberfill

SHOE STUFFERS CUTTING INSTRUCTIONS

From blue and cream check, cut:
※ 4 templates on page 112 (Note that the template includes a ¼" seam allowance)

From blue print, cut:
※ 2 – 1½" x 4" rectangles for bands

From assorted colored prints, cut:
※ 16 – 1½" squares

From raspberry print, cut:
※ Button cover fabrics, according to the instructions in the cover button kit

SHOE STUFFERS SEWING INSTRUCTIONS

1. Sew together 4 – 1½" colored print squares side by side. Repeat three times to create a total of four strips. Then sew these strips to the top straight edge of the 4 blue and cream check pieces cut from the template.

2. With right sides together, sew together two of the units created in Step 1, leaving the top straight edge open for stuffing later. Turn right side out.

3. Turn under the top edge a ¼", then another ¼" to hide raw edges. Then slipstitch the edge to the previous sewing line.

4. Right sides together, fold the 1½" x 4" blue print bands in half so they measure ¾" x 4". Then sew along one short end and the long side. Clip the corner and turn the bands right side out.

5. Following the instructions of your cover button kit, cover the buttons with the raspberry print fabric.

6. Fill the shoe stuffer with polyester fiberfill. Then wrap the blue print bands around the top edge of the stuffer, gathering the fabric. Overlap the band by a half inch, then attach a fabric-covered button to this and secure the two ends of the band. Repeat for the second shoe stuffer.

7. Insert the stuffers into your shoes and they will look as good as new on any adventure you take.

Eye Mask

Finished size: 3½" x 7½" • Designed and made by Anni Downs

My husband is a night owl whose greatest joy is to read in bed. I love him dearly but his nighttime bedside light is another matter. The invention of the eye mask has proven to be the perfect solution. It is amazing how much light it blocks out. Thanks to it, I can sleep soundly while he reads the night away.

FABRIC REQUIREMENTS
* 1 fat eighth blue dot
* ¼ yard lightweight fusible fleece
* DMC embroidery floss: White (Blanc), Light brown (167), Brown (869), Blue (926),
* Green (3012), and Raspberry (3721)
* 1 yard white hat elastic
* Template plastic

CUTTING INSTRUCTIONS
From blue dot, cut:
❄ 2 – 5" x 9" rectangles

From hat elastic, cut:
❄ Two 14"-long pieces

From fusible fleece, cut:
❄ One 5" x 9" piece

From template plastic, cut:
❄ One template on page 77 (Be sure to include the hat elastic markings on the template)

SEWING INSTRUCTIONS
1. Referring to the template's stitchery guide on page 77, trace the words and flowers centrally on the blue dot print with a fine Pigma pen. Do **not** draw or cut the eye mask shape at this time.

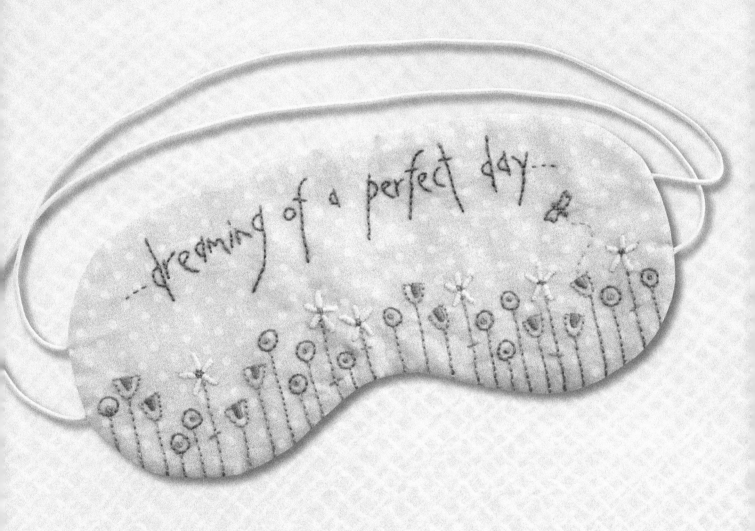

2. Using two strands of embroidery floss, stitch the following design elements:
   Words: DMC 869 (backstitch)
   Stems: DMC 3012 (backstitch)
   Tulip outlines: DMC 926 (backstitch)
   Tulip centers: DMC 167 (satin stitch)
   Circle flower outlines: DMC 3721 (backstitch)
   Circle flower centers: DMC 3012 (French knots)
   Daisy petals: DMC Blanc (satin stitch)
   Daisy centers: DMC 167 (French knots)
   Butterfly wings: DMC 3721 (backstitch)
   Butterfly body: DMC 167 (backstitch)
3. Using one strand of DMC 926 embroidery floss and a running stitch, sew the butterfly flight line.
4. Trace the template on the wrong side of the blue dot eye mask front. The drawn line is the sewing line, not the cutting line. Mark the hat elastic points on your fabric.

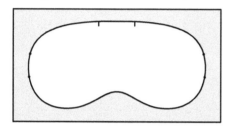

5. Position the 2 – 14" lengths of hat elastic at the points marked on the blue dot print so the ends extend a half inch from the drawn line.

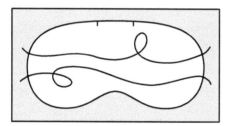

6. Iron the 5" x 9" fusible fleece to the wrong side of the blue dot eye mask back.

7. With right sides together, pin the blue dot eye mask back to the blue dot eye mask front, sandwiching the hat elastic. With the exception of the ends, make sure the length of hat elastic stays within the drawn perimeters of the eye mask so that no elastic gets caught while sewing.

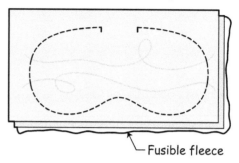

Fusible fleece

8. Using a small machine stitch, sew on the drawn line, leaving a small opening at the top for turning right side out. Sew over the elastic ends a few times to secure.
9. Trim an ⅛" seam allowance. Turn the eye mask right side out and slipstitch the opening closed. Place the mask over your eyes and dream the night away.

Sewing line   Leave open for turning

...dreaming of a perfect day...

Elastic
attachment
points

Elastic
attachment
points

Eye Mask

Travel to anywhere...

Add a ¼" seam allowance

ROME
USA
ENGLAND
NZ

Cut 1

**Travel
Document
Holder**

Sewing line

Leave open for turning

Punchneedle Door Hanging

My Favorite Things Quilt
Patty Cakes Block

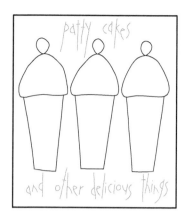

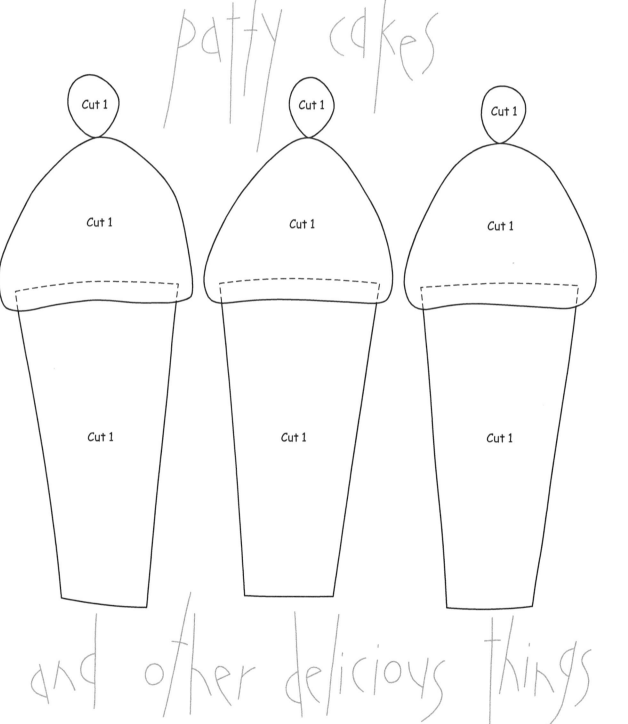

Cut 1

Cut 1

Cut 1

Cut 1

Cut 1

Cut 1

Cut 1

Cut 1

Cut 1

patty cakes

and other delicious things

My Favorite Things Quilt
Umbrella Block

Cut 1

singing in the rain

Cut 1

My Favorite Things Quilt
Tea Cup Block

Cut 1

Cut 1

Cut 1

Cut 1

Cut 1

My Favorite Things Quilt
Old Blue Jeans Block

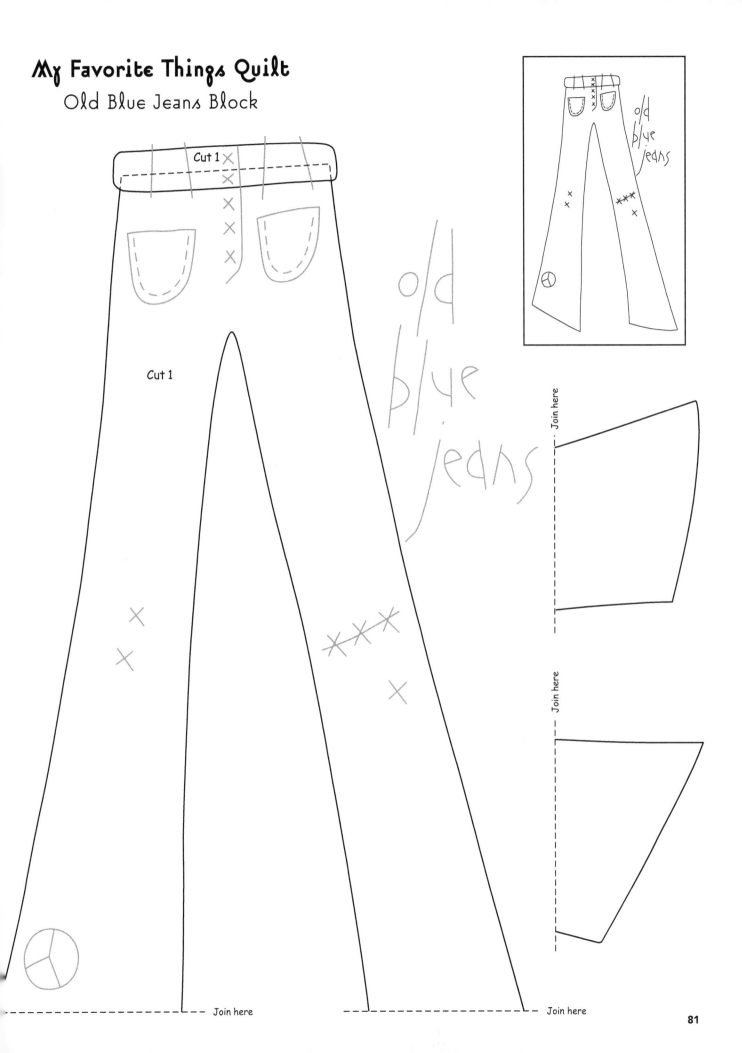

Cut 1

Cut 1

Join here

Join here

Join here

Join here

Join here

My Favorite Things Quilt
Suitcase Block

holidays

Cut 1

Cut 1

Cut 1

Cut 1

Cut 1

ROME

Cut 1

USA

Cut 1

ENGLAND

Cut 1

NZ

Cut 1

INTERNATIONAL

Cut 1

My Favorite Things Quilt
Chocolates Block

Cut 1

Cut 1

Cut 1

Cut 1

Cut 1

Cut 1

Cut 1

chocolates.... yum!

My Favorite Things Quilt
Title Block

my favorite things...

my favorite things...

My Favorite Things Quilt
Daisy Block

Cut 1

Cut 1

Cut 1

Cut 1

Join here – – – –

Join here – – – –

daisies

84

My Favorite Things Quilt
Ice Cream Block

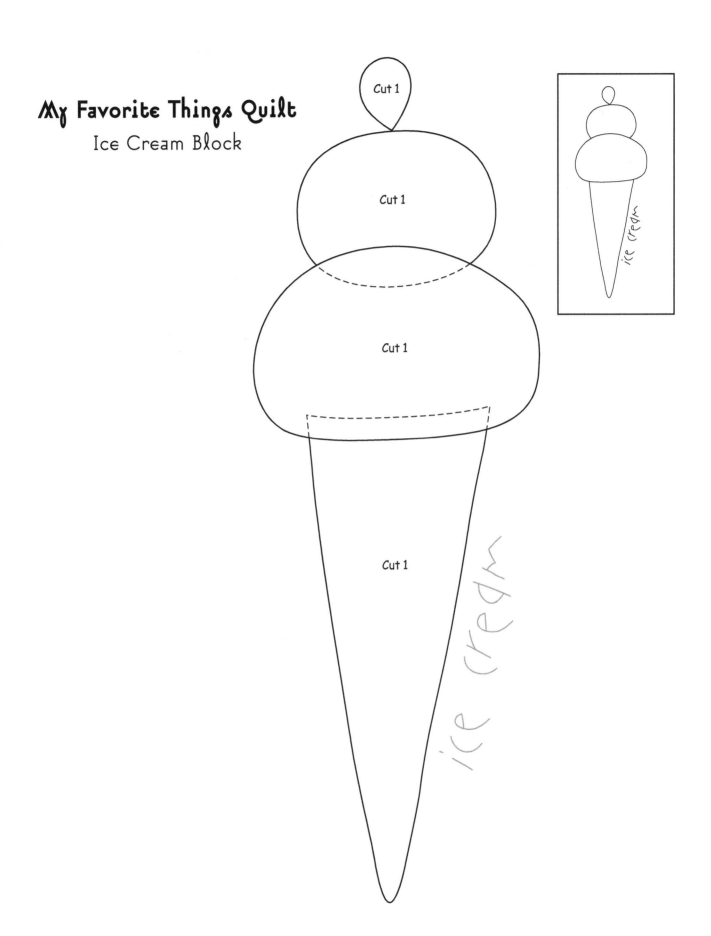

Cut 1

Cut 1

Cut 1

Cut 1

ice cream

ice cream

My Favorite Things Quilt
Hot Chocolate Block

Cut 1

Cut 1

My Favorite Things Quilt
Book Block

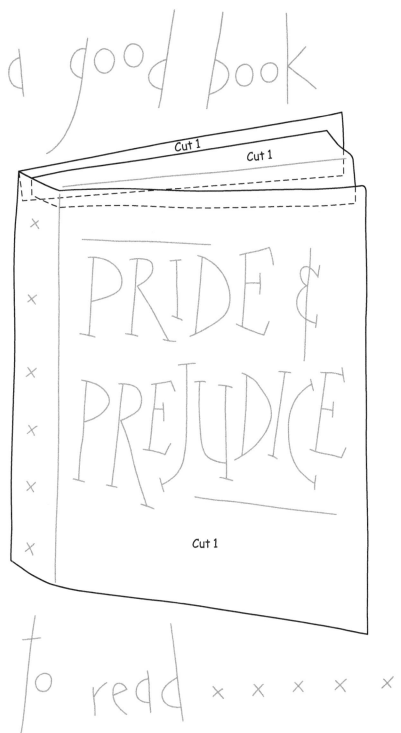

a good book

Cut 1

Cut 1

PRIDE &

PREJUDICE

Cut 1

to read × × × × ×

My Favorite Things Quilt
Home Block

Home

Cut 1

Cut 1

Cut 1

Cut 1

Cut 1

Cut 1

Join here

My Favorite Things Quilt
Home Block

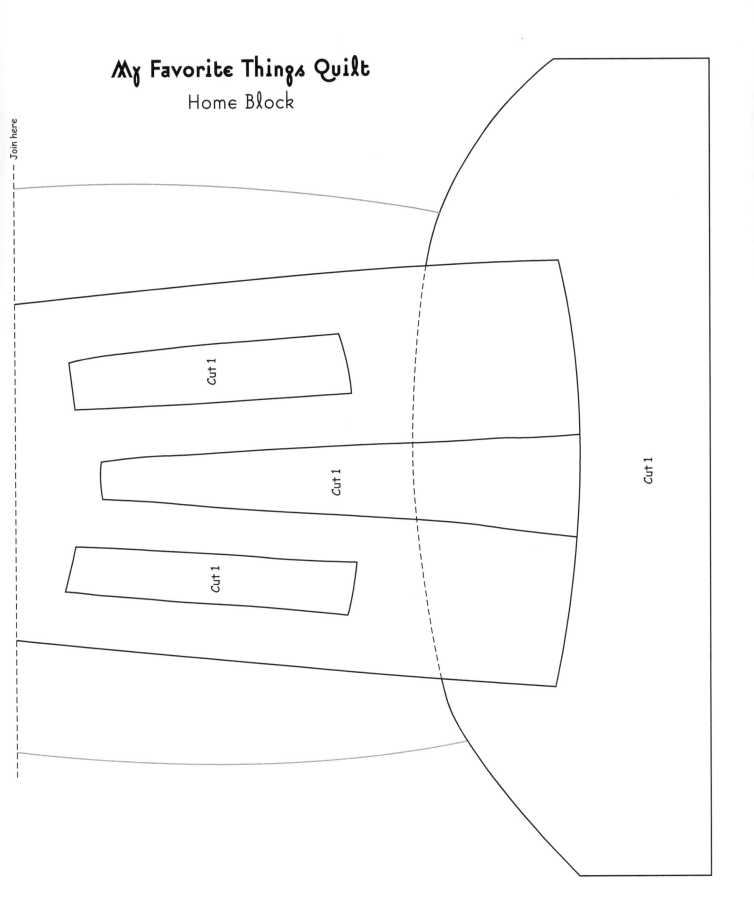

Join here

Cut 1

Cut 1

Cut 1

Cut 1

My Favorite Things Quilt
Flowers Block

gardening all day

Cut 1

Cut 1

Cut 1

Cut 1

Cut 1

Cut 1

Cut 1

Cut 1

Cut 1

Cut 1

Cut 1

Cut 1

Cut 1

Cut 1

Cut 1

Cut 1

Cut 1

Cut 1

Cut 1

gardening all day

My Favorite Things Quilt
Tree Block

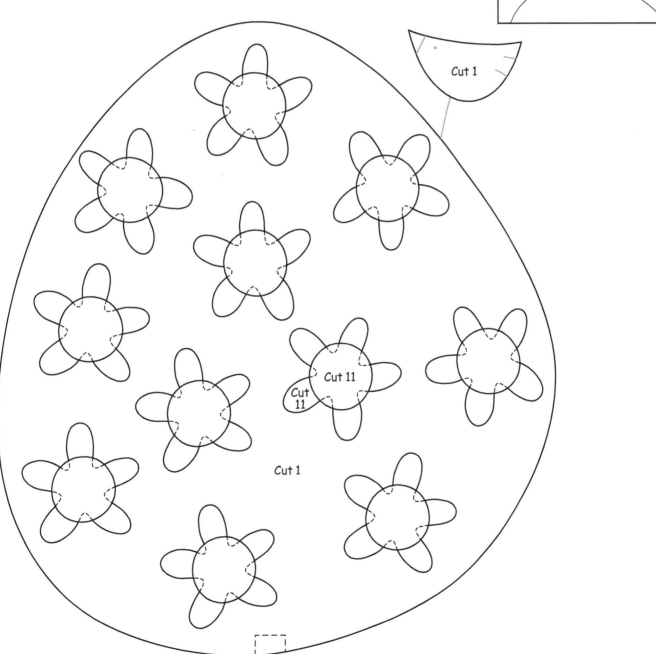

Cut 1

Cut 11

Cut 11

Cut 1

My Favorite Things Quilt
Tree Block

a tree to
sit under
and think

Cut
1

Cut 1

Cut 1

My Favorite Things Quilt
Rainbow Block

Cut 1

Cut 1

Cut 1

Cut 1

Cut 1

Cut 1

rainbows after rain

My Favorite Things Quilt
Sewing Block

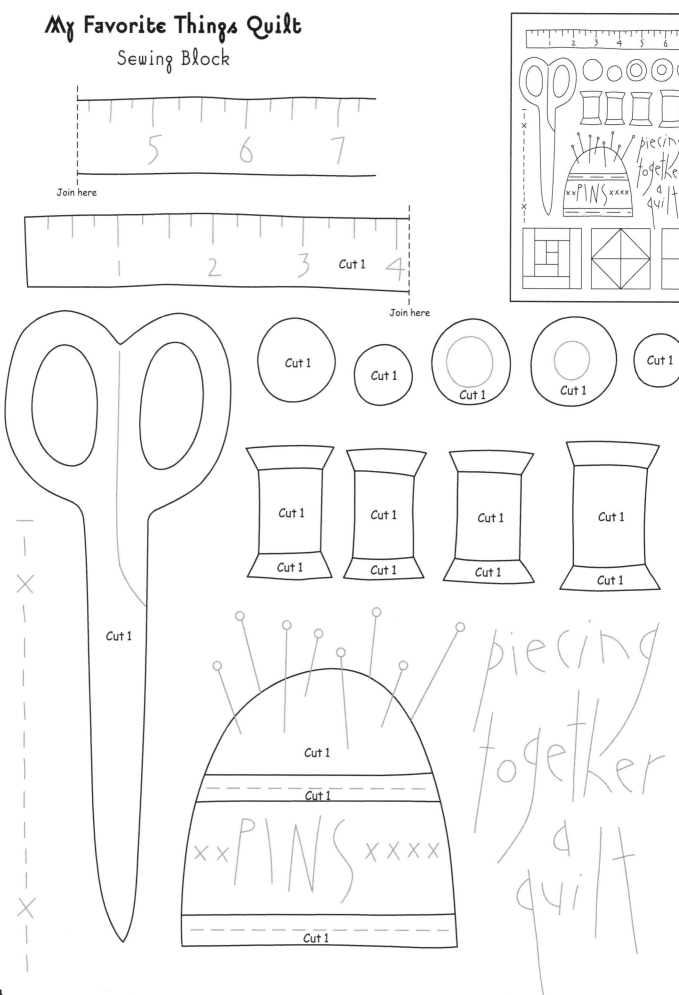

5 6 7

Join here

1 2 3 Cut 1 4

Join here

Cut 1

Cut 1 Cut 1 Cut 1 Cut 1 Cut 1

Cut 1 Cut 1 Cut 1 Cut 1

Cut 1 Cut 1 Cut 1 Cut 1

Cut 1

Cut 1

Cut 1

xx PINS xxxx

Cut 1

piecing togetker a quilt

My Favorite Things Quilt
Best Friends Block

best friends

Cut 1 Cut 1

Cut 1 Cut 1

Cut 1

—— Join here

My Favorite Things Quilt
Best Friends Block

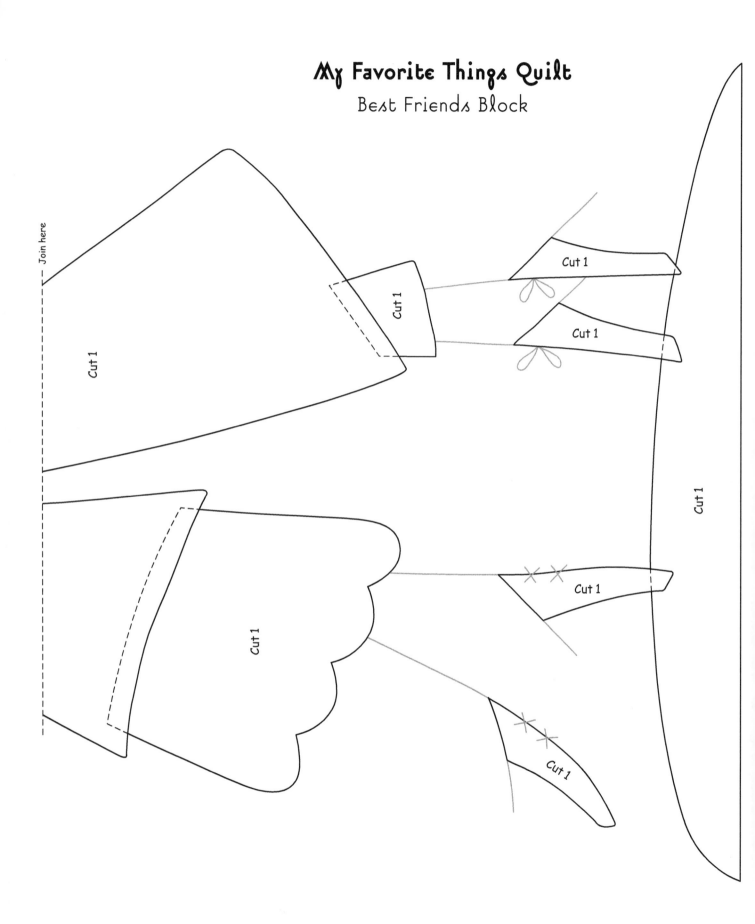

Join here

Cut 1

Cut 1

Cut 1

Cut 1

Cut 1

Cut 1

Cut 1

My Favorite Things Quilt
Shoes Block

simply gorgeous shoes

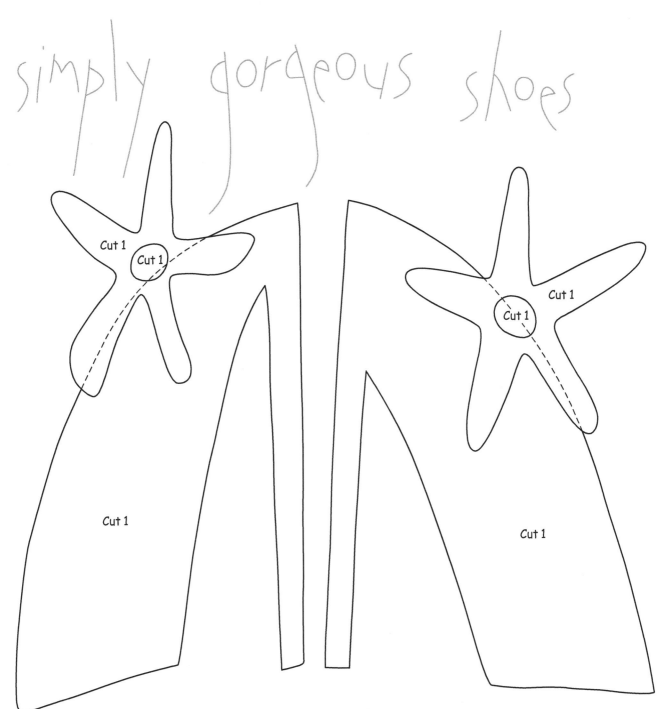

Cut 1

Cut 1

Cut 1

Cut 1

Cut 1

Cut 1

Cut 1

Cut 1

My Favorite Things Quilt
Cat Block

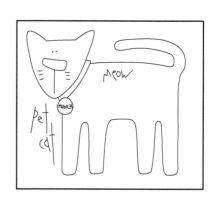

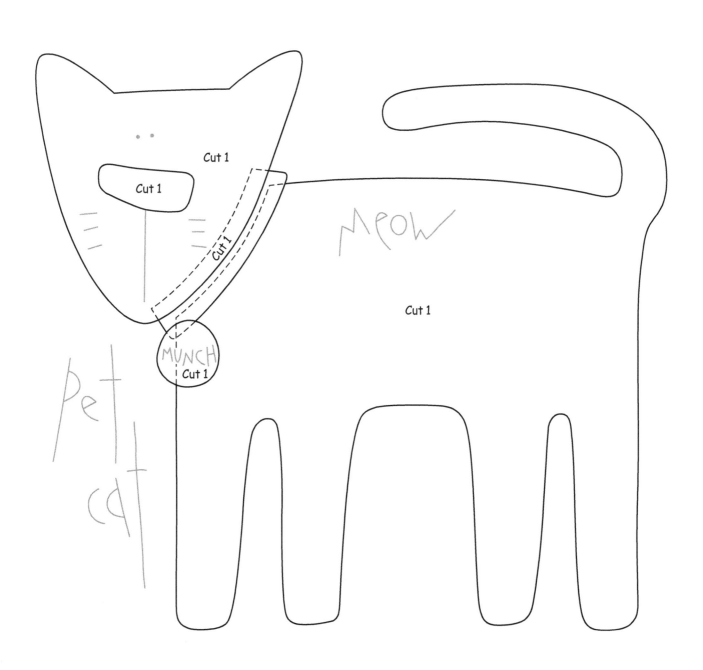

Cut 1

Cut 1

Cut 1

MUNCH
Cut 1

Meow

Cut 1

Pet cat

My Favorite Things Quilt
Butterfly Block

Cut 1

Cut 1

Cut 1

butterflies fluttering

My Favorite Things Quilt
Bird Block

Cut
1

Cut 1

Cut 1

birdsong in the morning

My Favorite Things Quilt
Sun Block

Cut 1

My Favorite Things Quilt
Chair Block

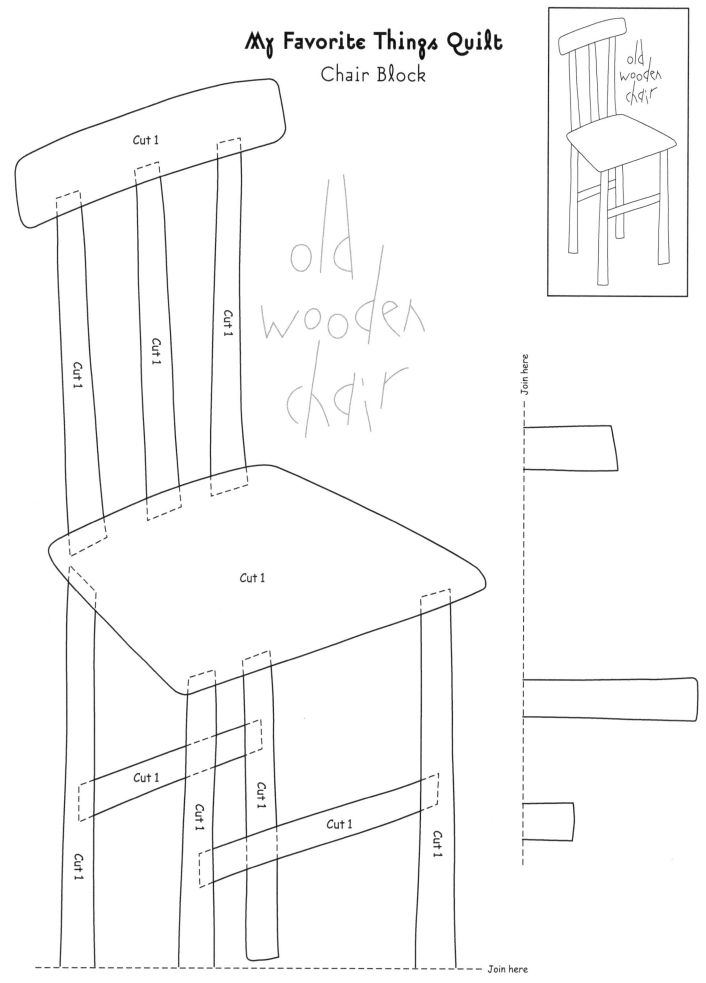

old wooden chair

Cut 1

Cut 1

Cut 1

Cut 1

Cut 1

Cut 1

Cut 1

Cut 1

Cut 1

Cut 1

Cut 1

Join here

Join here

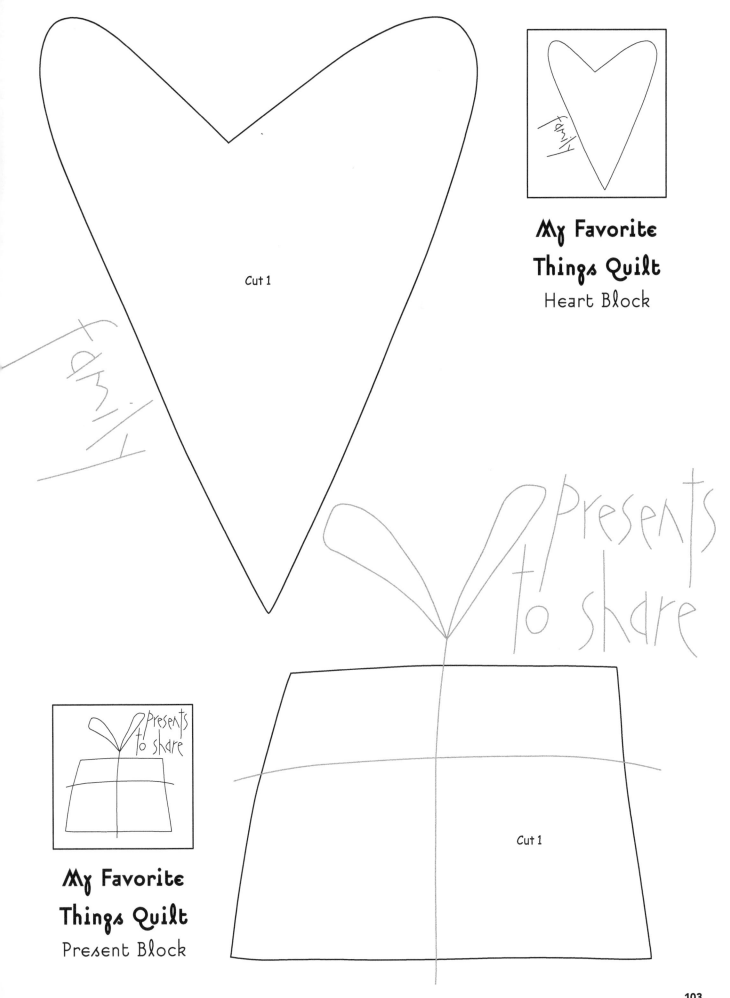

Cut 1

My Favorite Things Quilt
Heart Block

My Favorite
Things Quilt
Present Block

Cut 1

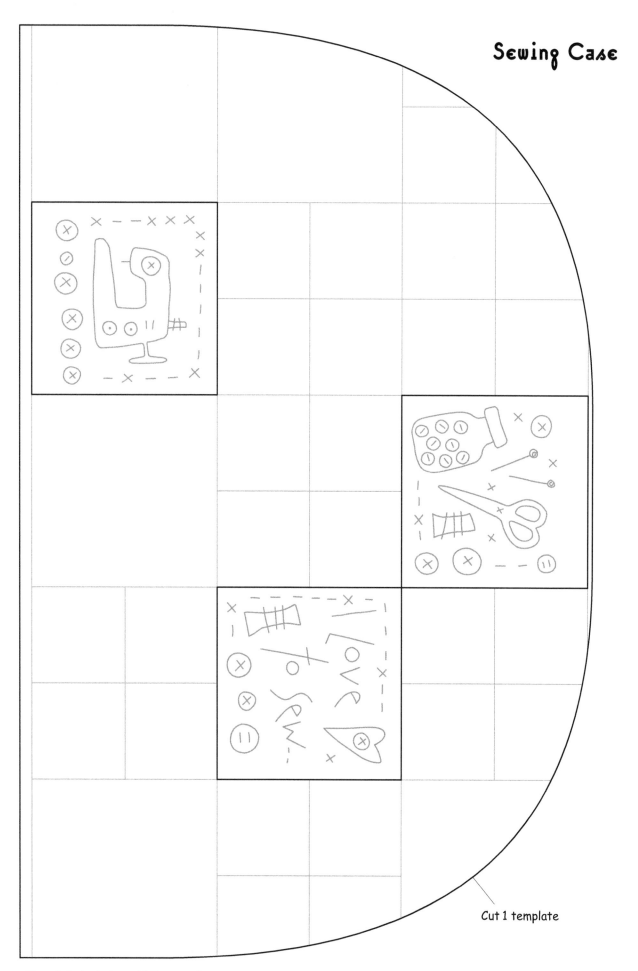

Sewing Case

Cut 1 template

Template includes a ¼" seam allowance

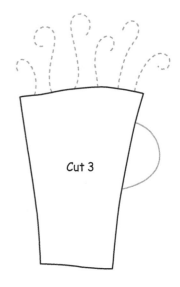

Table Runner

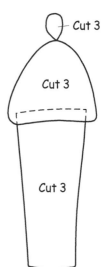

Cut 3

Cut 3

Cut 3

This template includes a ¼" seam allowance

Cut 1

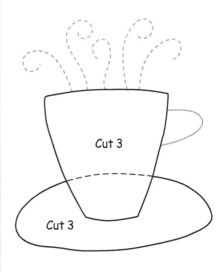

Cut 3

Cut 3

Needle Book

Cut 1 from cream fabric
Cut 1 from wool

Add a ¼" seam allowance to cream fabric only

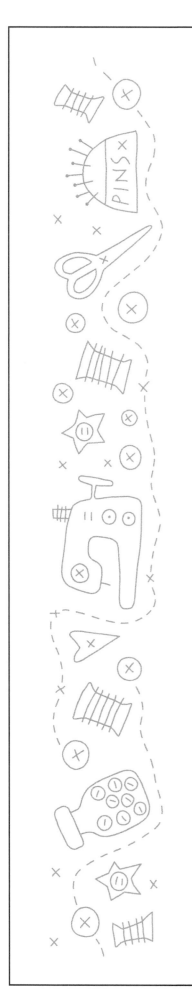

Pincushion

Cut 1

This template includes a 1/4" seam allowance

Pincushion
Top and Bottom

Cut 1 template

The drawn line is the sewing line

Pillow
Button
Flap

Pillow Bird Eye and
Eye Center Templates

Heat Bag

Cut 2

Bag Front & Back

Bag Front
& Back

Bag Gusset

Cut 1 template

Do not cut the fabric out along the base line

Lining

Cut 2

Cut 2

These templates include a ¼" seam allowance

Coin
Purse

*I love to shop for shoes, dresses, sunglasses, chocolate, handbags, perfume, cupcakes, shoes ♡, nail polish, lip stick, hats, shoes, books, music, presents for friends, shoes, cups of coffee

Shoe Bag

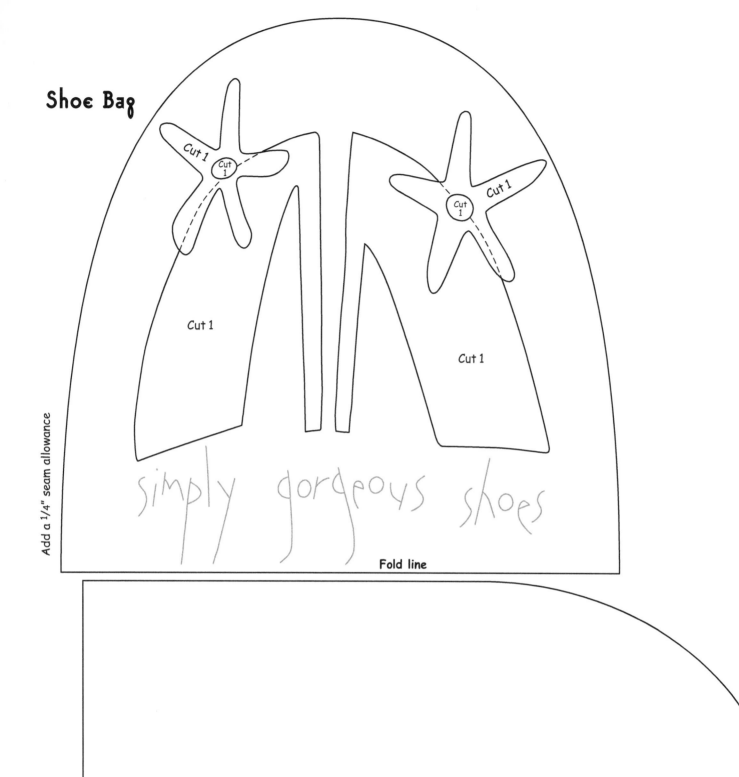

Cut 1

Cut 1
Cut 1

Cut 1
Cut 1

Cut 1

Cut 1

simply gorgeous shoes

Fold line

Shoe Stuffer
Cut 2 for each Stuffer

This template includes a 1/4" seam allowance

CPSIA information can be obtained
at www.ICGtesting.com
Printed in the USA
BVHW02s0908250918
528439BV00037B/1970/P